Basic accounting 1

Tutorial

David Cox

Michael Fardon

osborne
BOOKS

Published by Osborne Books Limited
Unit 1B Everoak Estate
Bromyard Road
Worcester WR2 5HP
Tel 01905 748071
Email books@osbornebooks.co.uk
Website www.osbornebooks.co.uk

Design by Laura Ingham
Cover and page design image © Istockphoto.com/Petrovich9

Printed by CPI Antony Rowe Limited, Chippenham

British Library Cataloguing in Publication Data
A catalogue record for this book is available from the British Library

ISBN 978 1905777 242

Contents

Acknowledgements

The publisher wishes to thank the following for their help with the reading and production of the book: Mike Gilbert and Jean Cox. Thanks are also due to Roger Petheram for his technical editorial work and to Laura Ingham for her designs for this series.

The publisher is indebted to the Association of Accounting Technicians for its help and advice to our authors and editors during the preparation of this text.

Authors

David Cox has more than twenty years' experience teaching accountancy students over a wide range of levels. Formerly with the Management and Professional Studies Department at Worcester College of Technology, he now lectures on a freelance basis and carries out educational consultancy work in accountancy studies. He is author and joint author of a number of textbooks in the areas of accounting, finance and banking.

Michael Fardon has extensive teaching experience of a wide range of banking, business and accountancy courses at Worcester College of Technology. He now specialises in writing business and financial texts and is General Editor at Osborne Books. He is also an educational consultant and has worked extensively in the areas of vocational business curriculum development.

Introduction

what this book covers

This book has been written specifically to cover Learning Area 'Basic Accounting I' which combines three QCF Units in the AAT Level 2 Certificate in Accounting:

- Principles of recording and processing financial transactions
- Preparing and recording financial documentation
- Processing ledger transactions and extracting a trial balance

The book contains a clear text with worked examples and case studies, chapter summaries and key terms to help with revision. Each chapter has a wide range of activities, many in the style of the computer-based assessments used by AAT.

This book covers the areas of financial documents and the theory and practice of double-entry. AAT has recommended that the Learning Area 'Basic Accounting I' should be covered before 'Basic Accounting II' which features the areas of control accounts, journals and trial balance adjustments. This second Learning Area, which has a separate assessment, is covered by Osborne Books' *Basic Accounting 2*.

Downloadable blank documents for use with this text are available in the Resources section of www.osbornebooks.co.uk

Osborne Workbooks

Osborne Workbooks contain practice material which helps students achieve success in their assessments. *Basic Accounting 1 Workbook* contains a number of paper-based 'fill in' practice exams in the style of the computer-based assessment. Please telephone the Osborne Books Sales Office on 01905 748071 for details of mail ordering, or visit the 24-hour online shop at www.osbornebooks.co.uk

International Accounting Standards (IAS) terminology

In this book the terms set out below are quoted as follows when they first appear in a chapter (and elsewhere where it seems appropriate):

> IAS terminology (UK terminology), ie
> receivables (debtors)
> payables (creditors)
> inventory (stock)
> non-current assets (fixed assets)

1 Introduction to the accounting system

this chapter covers...

This chapter is a basic introduction to the accounting system of a business and gives an overview of all the topics that will be explained throughout this book.

You may have a general idea of how accounting and finance 'fit into' a business and the reasons why money transactions are critical to its operation, but if you are working in an accounting and finance environment it is important to appreciate fully the way accounting systems work. It is the aim of the course you are studying that you will acquire the knowledge and skills which will enable you to work effectively in an accounting and finance environment.

This chapter describes and explains the basic structure of an accounting system. It covers:

- *the range of financial transactions in business, eg buying, selling, making payments*

- *the way in which financial documents such as invoices are used to record financial transactions*

- *the ways in which financial transactions are first recorded in the books of the business – using 'books of prime entry', eg a cash book*

- *the ways in which an accounting system is set up in a business, for example a double-entry system using ledger accounts*

- *the way in which the accounts are brought together in a summary known as the 'trial balance'*

- *the ways in which an accounting system can be used to provide information for the business owners and management, for example how much is owed by customers and how much profit has been made*

FINANCIAL TRANSACTIONS

All businesses carry out a wide range of financial transactions on a daily basis. These transactions will need documenting and then recording in some form of manual or computerised accounting system. Common transactions include:

selling goods and services

Goods and services can be sold:

- either for immediate payment – known as 'cash' sales, although confusingly this word 'cash' can involve payment by credit or debit card as well as notes and coins, or
- for payment at a later date – these are known as 'credit' sales

making purchases and paying expenses

Examples of purchases and expenses include a wide range of large and small transactions, some more important than others:

- settling purchase invoices, eg paying by cheque or by bank transfer for goods or services supplied during the previous month
- buying an item used in the business, eg a new delivery van, paid for with a cheque
- buying diesel fuel for the delivery van, using the company credit card
- buying some postage stamps for the office using cash

payments in and out of the bank account

The money received by the business and the money paid out by the business will pass through the bank account, for example:

- cash and cheques received from selling goods and services, paid over the counter into the bank account
- settling the company credit card by direct debit payment from the bank account
- paying the weekly wages through the bank account
- drawing cash out of the bank for use in the office

the importance of keeping track

As you will see from the above examples, recording financial transactions will be a complex process. A business will need to keep track of:

- expenses and purchases
- wages paid

- what each customer owes, and when the money is due
- amounts owed to suppliers, and when the payment is due
- amounts paid into the bank and out of the bank

If these transactions are not recorded accurately, the owner of the business and other interested organisations such as the bank and the tax authorities will not know how much money the business is making (or losing!).

THE FIVE STAGE ACCOUNTING SYSTEM

The accounting system, which will be set in motion by all the transactions listed on the previous page, can be broken down into five stages. These will be covered in greater detail later in this chapter. These stages (illustrated on the next page) are:

1 A **financial transaction** take place – a sale, a purchase, a payment

2 The transaction involves a **financial document**, for example an invoice (a sale), a credit note (returned goods), a cheque (payments), a petty cash voucher (small cash payments).

3 The document is first recorded on paper (or on computer) by the business, for example a 'day book' (for credit transactions) recording sales of goods or goods returned, a cash book recording payments in and out of the bank, or a petty cash book which records small cash payments made (eg buying some stamps for the office).

   These books are known as the **books of prime entry**; this simply means 'the first place a transaction is recorded in the accounting records.'

4 The entries in the books of prime entry, eg the day books, will then need to be transferred to the **ledger accounts** of the business. These are a formal record of the financial transactions and normally involve **double-entry accounts.**

   The double-entry system, which involves two entries for each transaction, a debit entry and a credit entry, is explained in more detail on pages 7-9.

5 The final stage in the accounting system covered on your course is the **trial balance**. This is a list of the balances of the double-entry accounts. It is used as a check on the accuracy of the account entries and is also a source of information for the business owners and managers: it will enable them to monitor items such as expenses and what their customers owe, and also to calculate how much profit the business has made. The trial balance is explained in more detail on page 10.

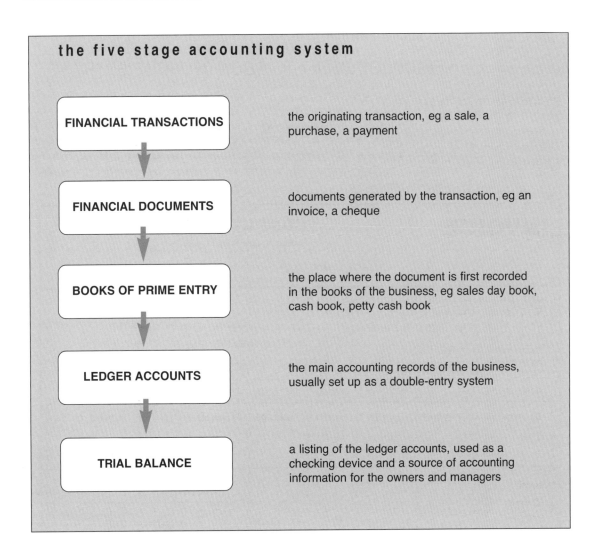

the five stage accounting system

FINANCIAL TRANSACTIONS — the originating transaction, eg a sale, a purchase, a payment

FINANCIAL DOCUMENTS — documents generated by the transaction, eg an invoice, a cheque

BOOKS OF PRIME ENTRY — the place where the document is first recorded in the books of the business, eg sales day book, cash book, petty cash book

LEDGER ACCOUNTS — the main accounting records of the business, usually set up as a double-entry system

TRIAL BALANCE — a listing of the ledger accounts, used as a checking device and a source of accounting information for the owners and managers

We will now explain the last four of these five stages in more detail. The first stage, financial transactions, has already been covered on page 3.

FROM DOCUMENTS TO BOOKS OF PRIME ENTRY

You will need to study a wide variety of financial documents as part of your course. On the next page a Case Study shows how a sales invoice – a **financial document** – is recorded in the sales day book, which is a list of sales invoices issued and a **book of prime entry**. You do not at this stage need to learn all the details of how this record is entered. This will be covered later.

Case Study

1.850

FROM DOCUMENT TO BOOK OF PRIME ENTRY

situation

Your business, Computrade, has sold a laptop computer to R S George Limited, for £564.00 (which is list price of £480 plus £84.00 VAT). The financial document issued here is a sales invoice (see below) which requires payment in 30 days' time. The details from this invoice are recorded in a sales day book (see bottom of the page), a book of prime entry.

INVOICE

COMPUTRADE

Ardent House, Mercia Way
Newtown, NT1 6TF
Tel 01722 295875 Fax 01722 295611 Email sales@computrade.com
VAT Reg GB 02756 6865 06

invoice to		
R S George Limited Unit 32 Bruges Trading Estate Winter Road Maidstone ME7 2PH	invoice no	2984
	account	8934
	your reference	CT524
	date/tax point	02 04 20-3

description	quantity	price	unit	total
Extreme 2120 Laptop	1	480.00	each	480.00

terms
30 days
E & OE

goods total	480.00
VAT	84.00
TOTAL	564.00

Sales Day Book					
Date	Customer	Invoice No.	Total	VAT	Net
20-3			£	£	£
2 April	R S George Limited	2984	564.00	84.00	480.00

FROM BOOKS OF PRIME ENTRY TO LEDGER ACCOUNTS

The next stage in the accounting system is the transfer of entries in the **books of prime entry** to the **ledger accounts**.

Examples of books of prime entry include:

- **day books** for credit sales and sales returns and credit purchases and purchases returns (see previous page for an example of a sales day book)
- **cash book** for recording payments into and out of the bank account

These will all be dealt with in detail in later chapters of this book.

The ledger accounts are the formal bookkeeping records kept by the business and are kept either in written form or on computer. Two written ledger accounts are illustrated below. This example shows payment of the invoice illustrated on the previous page. The amount due (£564), has been paid by R S George Limited, by cheque. It is recorded in the cash book, a book of prime entry, and then in two ledger accounts:

- bank account (a debit entry)
- the account of R S George Limited (a credit entry)

These accounts are shown here to illustrate the accounting system at work. Do not worry at this stage about how debits and credits work; this will be covered in full in Chapter 3.

Case Study

TRANSFER TO THE LEDGER ACCOUNTS

Computrade has sold a laptop computer to R S George Limited for £564.00. When payment by cheque is made a month later, it will be recorded in the cash book (book of prime entry) and the ledger accounts will record the transaction as follows:

Debit				Bank Account		Credit	
20-3	Details	£	p	20-3	Details	£	p
3 May	R S George Limited	564	00				

Debit				R S George Limited Account		Credit	
20-3	Details	£	p	20-3	Details	£	p
				3 May	Bank	564	00

THE LEDGER

In this chapter so far we have seen that the accounting system of a business records information from financial transactions and documents (such as invoices and cheques) into the books of prime entry and then into ledger accounts. It is useful at this point to explain:

- what is meant by 'the ledger'
- the way in which manual and computerised accounting systems organise 'the ledger'

Most businesses use an accounting system based on the **double-entry book-keeping system**, whereby each financial transaction is recorded in the accounts **twice**. This is shown in action at the bottom of the previous page where a payment received is recorded both in the bank account and also in the account of a customer who has made a payment. Book-keeping records are usually kept in one of two forms: handwritten (manual) records or on a computer system such as Sage.

the ledger – handwritten accounts

Handwriting the accounts is the traditional method of keeping 'the books,' particularly by smaller businesses. It is relatively straightforward and cheap to operate. The main record is the **ledger** – a large book into which each business transaction is entered by hand into individual **accounts**.

division of the ledger

Because of the potentially large number of accounts involved, the ledger is split up into different individual ledgers, both in manual systems and also in computer systems:

- **Sales ledger** – each customer is given a personal account which contains records of sales made on credit (ie buy now, pay later), any returned goods and payments received. This account shows the business the amount owed by that particular customer (a receivable).

- **Purchases ledger** – each supplier is given a personal account which contains records of purchases made on credit (ie buy now, pay later), any returned goods and payments made to the supplier. This account shows the amount owed to that particular supplier (a payable).

- **General ledger** – this collection of accounts records all other transactions of the business, such as

  - assets – these are things owned, eg premises, cars, computers
  - liabilities (items owed), eg overdrafts and bank loans
  - the owner's capital (the amount invested in the business by the owner)

- expense items – money going out, eg wages and rent paid
- income items – money coming in, eg sales and rent received

The *general ledger* is sometimes also known as the 'nominal' ledger (as in Sage computer accounting programs).

The 'ledger' structure is shown in the diagram at the bottom of the page.

control accounts

Many businesses use **control accounts** to provide them with information about the financial state of the organisation.

Control accounts are 'total' accounts which summarise a number of other accounts. They are set out in the same way as all other ledger accounts. Examples include:

- **sales ledger control account** which contains the totals of all the receivable (debtor) accounts in the sales ledger – this tells the business how much is owing from all their customers, a figure that is important for business owners and managers

- **purchases ledger control account** which contains the totals of all the payable (creditor) accounts in the purchases ledger – this tells the business how much is owing to all their suppliers at any one time; again this is a figure that is important for anyone running a business

These control accounts are always contained in the general ledger. It is the total of these accounts that is transferred to the trial balance (see next page).

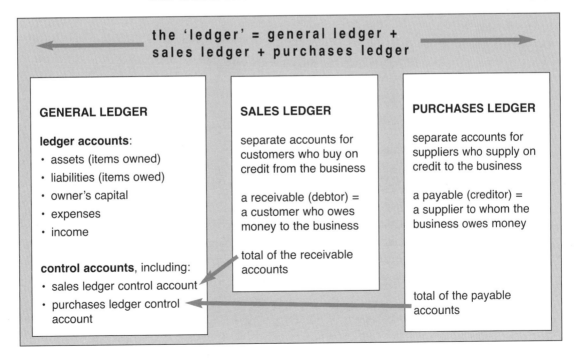

the 'ledger' = general ledger +
sales ledger + purchases ledger

GENERAL LEDGER

ledger accounts:
- assets (items owned)
- liabilities (items owed)
- owner's capital
- expenses
- income

control accounts, including:
- sales ledger control account
- purchases ledger control account

SALES LEDGER

separate accounts for customers who buy on credit from the business

a receivable (debtor) = a customer who owes money to the business

total of the receivable accounts

PURCHASES LEDGER

separate accounts for suppliers who supply on credit to the business

a payable (creditor) = a supplier to whom the business owes money

total of the payable accounts

THE TRIAL BALANCE

format of a trial balance

A trial balance is the important final stage in the accounting system. It brings together the balances of all the ledger accounts in the general ledger, setting them out in two columns – a debit column and a credit column – which when added up should show two equal totals.

A simplified trial balance is shown on the next page. You do not need at this stage to know how all this 'works' but just that it is an important accuracy check in the accounting system.

Note that the trial balance is headed up with

- the **name** of the business, 'Computrade'
- the **date** on which it was drawn up – this should be done regularly, eg the end of each month, and always the end of the financial year

what the trial balance shows

The trial balance shows the business owner and managers important and useful information. For example, the trial balance on the next page sets out the account balances of Computrade, it shows that:

- sales are £58,050

- £12,500 is owed by the customers (receivables)

- £9,350 is owed to suppliers (payables)

- the wages paid out totalled £44,100

- the delivery vans are worth £36,000

- the business has £2,000 in the bank

- the owner of the business has an investment (capital) worth £105,000

Note that the receivables and payables figures are 'total' figures and are taken from the sales ledger and purchases ledger control accounts. This makes the trial balance more manageable and meaningful – it would be rather difficult to list all the customer (receivable) and supplier (payable) accounts separately!

the trial balance

Name of business: Computrade
Trial Balance as at 30 June 20-3

	Debit	Credit
	£	£
Purchases	35,000	
Sales		58,050
Receivables	12,500	
Payables		9,350
Insurance	1,400	
Rent	6,400	
Wages	44,100	
Bank	2,000	
Office equipment	35,000	
Delivery vans	36,000	
Capital		105,000
	172,400	172,400

names of all the individual ledger accounts

totals of the two money amount columns – note that they add up to the same figure, providing an accuracy check of the accounting system

■ The accounting system is normally made up of five stages:

1 financial transactions

2 financial documents

3 books of prime entry

4 ledger accounts

5 trial balance

■ **Financial transactions** are the starting point of the accounting system. They include sales, purchases, expenses, payments in and out of the bank account and small cash (petty cash) transactions.

■ Financial transactions normally result in **financial documents**, for example an invoice (for a sale), a credit note (for returned goods), a cheque (for a payment), a petty cash voucher (for a small cash payment).

■ In the next stage of the accounting system financial documents are recorded in **books of prime entry**, for example separate day books for sales and sales returns, purchases and purchases returns, the cash book and the petty cash book.

■ Next the **ledger accounts** are written up from the books of prime entry. The ledger accounts are normally double-entry accounts, ie two entries are made in the accounts for each transaction – a debit entry and a credit entry.

■ As there are so many ledger accounts, **the ledger** is often split into separate ledgers: sales ledger (for customer accounts), purchases ledger (for supplier accounts) and general ledger (all the other accounts, including assets, expenses, income, liabilities, and capital).

■ **Control accounts** are 'total' accounts used to summarise important groups of ledger accounts, eg sales ledger control account.

■ Finally, the balances of the ledger accounts are transferred to the **trial balance** which is both a checking device and also a source of accounting information for the business owners and managers.

■ The format of a trial balance presents the ledger accounts in two columns – one for debit balances and one for credit balances. The totals of the two columns should agree, providing an accuracy check of the accounting system.

Key Terms		
	financial document	a term given to a document which results from a financial transaction, eg an invoice
	'cash' and 'credit' sales	a 'cash' sale is a sale where payment is made straightaway, a 'credit' sale is a sale where payment is made at a later date
	books of prime entry	the place in the books of a business where a financial transaction is recorded for the first time, eg day books, cash book, petty cash book
	day books	a book of prime entry which lists the details of various financial transactions, eg sales, sales returns, purchases and purchases returns
	cash book	the book of prime entry which lists payments in and out of the bank account
	petty cash book	the book of prime entry which lists small cash (notes and coins) business expense payments from an office cash fund
	ledger account	the formal accounting record (often in double-entry format) for financial transactions involving individuals (customers and suppliers) and business assets, expenses, income, liabilities and capital
	double-entry accounts	ledger accounts set up on the double-entry system (ie two entries – a debit and a credit – are made for each transaction)
	the ledger	means literally 'the book' which contains the individual accounts; it is often subdivided into different categories, eg sales ledger, purchases ledger, general ledger
	control accounts	'total' accounts contained in the general ledger
	receivable	a customer who owes a business money
	payable	a supplier owed money by a business
	assets	items owned by a business, eg a delivery van
	liabilities	items owed by a business, eg a bank loan
	capital	the investment made in a business by the owner(s), ie the amount owed to the owner(s) by the business
	trial balance	a list of the balances of the ledger accounts drawn up in two columns (debit and credit) the totals of which should be the same

Activities

1.1   A 'cash sale' in accounting terms is:

   (a)   a sale involving notes and coins

   (b)   a sale requiring immediate payment

   (c)   a sale requiring payment in the future

   Which one of these options is correct?

1.2   A financial document is first recorded in an accounting system in a book of prime entry.
   True or false?

1.3   The following are all books of prime entry:

   (a)   cash book, petty cash book, purchases ledger

   (b)   sales day book, sales returns day book, sales ledger

   (c)   cash book, petty cash book, sales day book

   Which one of these options is correct?

1.4   Transactions recorded in the books of prime entry are then transferred to:

   (a)   ledger accounts

   (b)   a trial balance

   (c)   a petty cash book

   Which one of these options is correct?

1.5   A receivable is:

   (a)   a supplier owed money by the business

   (b)   a customer who owes money to a business

   (c)   a customer who settles straightaway using cash

   Which one of these options is correct?

1.6   In double-entry book-keeping every transaction is recorded using

   (a)   two debits

   (b)   two credits

   (c)   one debit and one credit

   Which one of these options is correct?

1.7   The purchases ledger contains the ledger accounts for

    (a)   receivables

    (c)   payables

    (c)   expenses

    Which one of these options is correct?

1.8   A liability of a business is:

    (a)   an amount owed by that business

    (b)   an item owned by that business

    (c)   a cash fund for business expenses

    Which one of these options is correct?

1.9   An extract from the trial balance of a shop that sells tiles is shown below.

Name of business: Style & Tile
Trial Balance as at 30 June 20-3 (extract)

	Debit £	Credit £
Receivables	10,500	
Payables		6,720
Advertising	1,400	
Insurance	780	
Wages	52,800	
Bank	3,000	
Shop equipment	22,000	
Delivery vans	28,000	
Capital		155,000

On the basis of the figures shown here, answer the following questions:

    (a)   How much do the customers of Style & Tile owe the business?

    (b)   How much does Style & Tile owe its suppliers?

    (c)   How much does Style & Tile have in the bank?

    (d)   How much investment does the owner have in the business?

    (e)   Where are the figures for Receivables and Payables taken from?

2 Financial documents for sales

This chapter examines the procedures involved when a business sells goods or services on credit – which means that payment is made at a later date, possibly a month later.

The important point here is that the business wants to get paid on time and it wants to get the right amount. It can achieve these aims through the efficient use and monitoring of financial documents.

This chapter covers the areas of:

- *the use of business documents – quotation, purchase order, invoice, delivery note, returns note, credit note, statement*

- *the calculation of document totals and discounts*

- *the calculation of Value Added Tax (VAT)*

- *the coding of documents*

- *the checking and authorisation of documents*

Note that the documents explained in this chapter illustrate the traditional paper-based system. There is nowadays a growing trend for electronic documents, eg online orders, invoices, statements and payments. These follow the same principles as the paper-based documents.

FINANCIAL DOCUMENTS

When a business sells goods or services it will use a number of different documents (listed in the diagram below). A single sales transaction of course involves both seller *and* buyer. In this chapter we look at the situation from the point of view of the *seller* of the goods or services. The transaction from the point of view of the buyer is dealt with in Chapter 5. Documents which are used in the *selling* process include:

• price **quotation** which the seller may be asked to provide

• **purchase order** which the seller receives from the buyer

• **delivery note** which goes with the goods from the seller to the buyer

• **invoice** which lists the goods and tells the buyer what is owed

• **returns note** which is sent with any goods that are being returned

• **credit note** which is sent to the buyer if any refund is due

• **statement** sent by the seller to remind the buyer what is owed

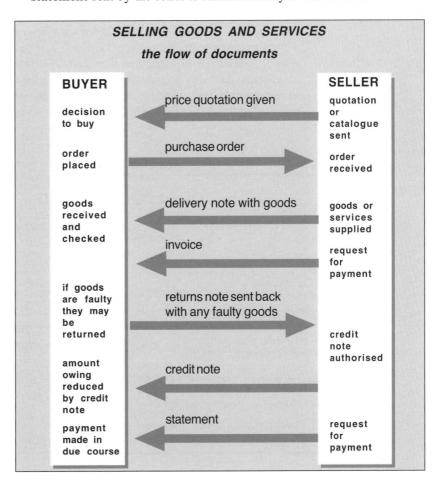

the flow of documents

Before you read the Case Study, make sure you have studied the diagram on the previous page. You will see in the columns representing the buyer and the seller that there are various activities requiring financial documents.

Case Study

1.850

1.600

COOL SOCKS – A SALES TRANSACTION

situation

Cool Socks Limited manufactures fashion socks in a variety of colours. It supplies a number of different customers, including Trends, a fashion store in Broadfield. In this Case Study, Trends places an order for 100 pairs of socks with Cool Socks. The socks are delivered, but some are found to be faulty, so some of the socks have to be returned. The Case Study looks in detail at the documents involved.

THE PRICE QUOTATION

Before placing the order, the buyer at Trends will need to find out the price of the socks. This can be done by consulting Cool Socks' catalogue, or by means of a written or telephoned enquiry, or, if Cool Socks has a website, by looking at the product pages or by making an on-line enquiry. Cool Socks *may* provide a written quotation for the socks if they are requested to do so, although this procedure is more common with higher value orders. A written quotation might look like this:

QUOTATION

COOL SOCKS LIMITED

Unit 45 Elgar Estate, Broadfield, BR7 4ER
Tel 01908 765314 Fax 01908 765951 Email toni@cool.u-net.com
VAT REG GB 0745 4672 76

Trends 4 Friar Street Broadfield BR1 3RF	date	19 09 20-3

Thank you for your enquiry of 17 September 20-3. We are pleased to quote as follows:

100 pairs Toebar socks (blue)@ £2.36 a pair, excluding VAT.

M Arnold

Sales Department

PURCHASE ORDER – THE SOCKS ARE ORDERED

The buyer at Trends, once she has accepted the quoted price will post or fax the authorised purchase order shown below, or she might send an online order. The order will have been processed manually, or produced on a computer accounting program.

Note the following details:

- each purchase order has a specific reference number (here it is 47609) – this is useful for filing and quoting on later documents such as invoices and statements; this reference number is an example of **coding** in accounting

- the catalogue number of the goods required is stated in the product code column – this number is a further example of **coding**; it includes a number and a letter

- the quantity of the goods required is stated in the quantity column – socks are obviously supplied in pairs!

- the description of the goods is set out in full

- the price is not needed, although some purchase orders will include a price

- the purchase order is signed and dated by the person in charge of purchasing – without this authorisation the supplier is unlikely to supply the goods (the order will probably be returned!)

Trends

4 Friar Street
Broadfield
BR1 3RF

Tel 01908 761234 Fax 01908 761987
VAT REG GB 0745 8383 56

PURCHASE ORDER

Cool Socks Limited,	purchase order no	47609
Unit 45 Elgar Estate,	date	25 09 20-3
Broadfield,		
BR7 4ER		

product code	quantity	description
45B	100 pairs	Blue Toebar socks

AUTHORISED   signature...........*D Signer*...date.........*25/09/20-3*

DELIVERY NOTE – THE SOCKS ARE DELIVERED

A delivery note is despatched with the goods when the order is ready. It is either processed manually in the office or printed out by a computer accounting program, often at the same time as the invoice (see next page). In this case, the delivery note travels with the socks, and a copy will be signed by Trends on receipt. Note the following details:

- the delivery note has a numerical reference (here it is 68873), useful for filing and later reference if there is a query – this is another example of coding

- the method of delivery is stated – here the delivery is by parcel carrier

- the delivery note quotes the purchase order number – 47609 – this enables the buyer to 'tie up' the delivery with the original purchase order – this is another example of the use of coding

- the delivery note quotes
  - Cool Socks' catalogue reference 45B as the product code
  - the quantity supplied
  - the description of the goods, but no price – it is not needed at this stage

  these details will be checked against the goods themselves straightaway so that any discrepancies can be reported without delay

- the delivery note will be signed and dated by the person receiving the goods as proof of delivery; nowadays this process can also be carried out electronically – the person receiving the goods will be asked to sign a portable electronic device

---

──── DELIVERY NOTE ────
COOL SOCKS LIMITED
Unit 45 Elgar Estate, Broadfield, BR7 4ER
Tel 01908 765314 Fax 01908 765951 Email toni@cool.u-net.com
VAT REG GB 0745 4672 76

Trends 4 Friar Street Broadfield BR1 3RF	delivery note no	68873
	delivery method	Lynx Parcels
	your order	47609
	date	02 10 20–3

product code	quantity	description
45B	100 pairs	Blue Toebar socks

Received

signature......*V Williams*......name (capitals)..*V WILLIAMS*......date..*6/10/20-3*

INVOICE – THE SELLER REQUESTS PAYMENT

The invoice is the trading document which is sent by the seller to the buyer stating how much is owed by the buyer of goods or services.

The invoice, like the delivery note, is prepared in the supplier's (seller's) office, and is either processed manually or produced on a computer printer using a computer accounting program.

Invoices produced by different organisations will vary to some extent in terms of detail, but their basic layout will always be the same. The invoice prepared by Cool Socks Limited – illustrated on page 23 – is typical of a modern typed or computer printed document.

An invoice will normally be printed as part of a multiple set of documents which is likely to include a delivery note and a copy invoice for the seller's own records. The copy invoice will normally be filed in numerical order (see 'coding' below). If a computer accounting program is used, the invoice can, of course, be called up on screen, referenced by its invoice number.

Note the following details, and refer to the invoice on page 23.

addresses

The invoice shows the address:

- of the seller of the goods – Cool Socks Limited
- where the invoice should be sent – to Trends
- where the goods are to be sent – if it is different from the invoice address

coding and references

There are a number of important coding references on the invoice:

- the numerical reference of the invoice itself – 787923
- the account number allocated to Trends by the seller – 3993 – for use in the seller's computer accounting program; sometimes account references can include letters as well
- the original reference number on the purchase order sent by Trends – 47609 – which will enable the shop to 'tie up' the invoice with the original order
- the product code from the seller's catalogue or product list – here it is 45B

Note that coding on a financial document can be:

- numeric – ie just numbers
- alpha-numeric – ie a mixture of letters and numbers

date

The date on the invoice is important because the payment date (here one month) is calculated from it. It is also the transaction date used for VAT (Value Added Tax) purposes (see the next page).

the goods

The invoice must specify accurately the goods supplied. The details – set out in columns in the body of the invoice – include:

- **product code** – this is the catalogue number which appeared on the original purchase order and on the delivery note

- **description** – the goods must be specified precisely

- **quantity** – this should agree with the quantity ordered

- **price** – this is the price of each unit shown in the next column

- **unit** is the way in which the unit is counted and charged for, eg 'boxes' of tights or single items, eg designer dresses, in which case the unit is quoted as 'each'

- **total** is the unit price multiplied by the number of units

- **discount %** is the percentage allowance (often known as 'trade' discount) given to customers who regularly deal with the supplier, ie they receive a certain percentage (eg 10%) deducted from their bill (see page 26 for further explanation of discounts)

- discounts are also given for **bulk purchases** – 'bulk discount' will also be shown in the discount column

- **net** is the amount due to the seller after deduction of trade or bulk discount, and before VAT is added on

totals and VAT

Further calculations are made in the box at the bottom of the invoice:

- **Goods Total** is the amount due to the seller (it is the total of the net column)

- **Value Added Tax (VAT)**, here calculated as 17.5% of the total after deduction of any cash discount. VAT is added to produce the invoice final total

- **Total** is the VAT plus the Goods Total; it is the amount due to the seller

Note: VAT (Value Added Tax) is a 'sales tax' on the supply of goods and services. It is changed from time-to-time by the Government. In this book a standard VAT rate of 17.5% is used.

terms

The terms of payment are stated on the invoice. In this case these include:

- **Net monthly** – this means that full payment of the invoice should be made within a month of the invoice date

- **Carriage paid** means that the price of the goods includes delivery

- **E & OE** stands for 'errors and omissions excepted' which means that if there is a error or something left off the invoice by mistake, resulting in an incorrect final price, the supplier has the right to rectify the mistake and demand the correct amount

Another term used (not shown here) is **Settlement Discount** (also known as **Cash Discount**) – a further discount given when payment is made early, eg '2.5% settlement discount for payment within 7 days'. See page 28 for further details.

━━ **INVOICE** ━━

COOL SOCKS LIMITED
Unit 45 Elgar Estate, Broadfield, BR7 4ER
Tel 01908 765314 Fax 01908 765951 Email toni@cool.u-net.com
VAT Reg GB 0745 4672 76

invoice to

| Trends |
| 4 Friar Street |
| Broadfield |
| BR1 3RF |

invoice no	787923
account	3993
your reference	47609
date/tax point	02 10 20-3

deliver to

as above

product code	description	quantity	price	unit	total	discount %	net
45B	Blue toebar socks	100	2.36	pair	236.00	0.00	236.00

terms
Net monthly
Carriage paid
E & OE

goods total	236.00
VAT	41.30
TOTAL	277.30

CREDIT NOTE – A REFUND IS DUE TO THE BUYER

A **credit note** is a 'refund' document. It reduces the amount owed by the buyer. The goods, remember, have not yet been paid for. The credit note is prepared by the seller and sent to the buyer. Examples of reasons for a refund by credit note include:

· the goods may have been damaged, lost in transit or they may be faulty

· not all the goods have been sent – this is referred to as 'shortages'

· the unit price on the invoice may be incorrect and the buyer overcharged

In this Case Study, when the staff of Trends unpack the socks in the store room they find that ten pairs are damaged. They telephone Cool Socks to report the problem and Cool Socks authorise the return of the socks for credit. These socks will then be sent back to Cool Socks with a request for credit – ie a reduction in the bill for the 10 damaged pairs – with a document known as a returns note (see page 97). Cool Socks will then issue the credit note for £27.73 shown below. Note the following details:

· the invoice number of the original consignment is quoted

· the reason for the issue of the credit note is stated at the bottom of the credit note – here 'damaged' goods

· the details are otherwise exactly the same as on an invoice

---

———— CREDIT NOTE ————
COOL SOCKS LIMITED
Unit 45 Elgar Estate, Broadfield, BR7 4ER
Tel 01908 765314 Fax 01908 765951 Email toni@cool.u-net.com
VAT REG GB 0745 4672 76

to

Trends
4 Friar Street
Broadfield
BR1 3RF

credit note no	12157
account	3993
your reference	47609
our invoice	787923
date/tax point	10 10 20–3

product code	description	quantity	price	unit	total	discount %	net
45B	Blue Toebar socks	10	2.36	pair	23.60	0.00	23.60

Reason for credit
10 pairs of socks received – damaged

GOODS TOTAL	23.60
VAT	4.13
TOTAL	27.73

STATEMENT – THE SELLER REQUESTS PAYMENT

A seller will not normally expect a buyer to pay each individual invoice as soon as it is received: this could result in the buyer having to make a number of payments during the month. Instead, a **statement of account** is sent by the supplier to the buyer at the end of the month.

This statement, which can be typed out, or printed by the seller's computer accounting program, shows what is owed by the buyer to the seller. It contains details of:

- any balances (amounts owing) at the beginning of the month – these appear in the debit column with the wording 'balance b/f' in the details column ('b/f' stands for 'brought forward')
- any payments received from the buyer (credit column)
- invoices issued for goods supplied – the full amount due, including VAT (debit column)
- refunds made on credit notes – including VAT (credit column)
- the running balance and, in the box at the bottom, the final net total of all the items

The statement issued by Cool Socks to Trends for the period covering the sale and refund is shown below. Note that the balance of £150 owing at the beginning of the month has been paid off in full by a cheque on 2 October.

STATEMENT OF ACCOUNT ——

COOL SOCKS LIMITED

Unit 45 Elgar Estate, Broadfield, BR7 4ER
Tel 01908 765314 Fax 01908 765951 Email toni@cool.u-net.com
VAT REG GB 0745 4672 76

TO

Trends
4 Friar Street
Broadfield
BR1 3RF

account   3993

date   31 10 20-3

date	details	debit £	credit £	balance £
01 10 20-3	Balance b/f	150.00		150.00
02 10 20-3	Cheque received		150.00	00.00
02 10 20-3	Invoice 787923	277.30		277.30
10 10 20-3	Credit note 12157		27.73	249.57

		TOTAL	249.57

DISCOUNTS

The invoice in the Case Study (see the opposite page) shows a column for **discount**.

We also saw that the terms at the bottom of the invoice can allow for **settlement discount** (also known as **cash discount**).

We will now explain these terms and show how the discount is calculated.

trade discount and bulk discount

It is common practice for suppliers to give businesses that order from them on a regular basis an agreed discount – a percentage reduction in the invoiced amount. This is known as **trade discount** because it applies to businesses 'in the trade' rather than to the general public. Discount may also be given by sellers to buyers who purchase in large quantities or over certain money amounts (eg over £5,000); this is known as **bulk discount**.

In the example on the next page 10% trade discount has been given to Trends. Note how the discount percentage is shown in the discount column and the net amount is the amount after deduction of the discount.

The calculations on the invoice are as follows:

Step 1	Calculate the total price before discount
	100 x £2.36 = £236.00
Step 2	Calculate the trade discount
	£236.00 x 10% (ie 10/100) = £23.60
Step 3	Calculate the net price before VAT
	£236.00 - £23.60 = £212.40
Step 4	Calculate the VAT
	£212.40 x 17.5% (ie 17.5/100) = £37.17
Step 5	Calculate the total invoice price
	£212.40 + £37.17 = £249.57

INVOICE

COOL SOCKS LIMITED

Unit 45 Elgar Estate, Broadfield, BR7 4ER
Tel 01908 765314 Fax 01908 765951 Email toni@cool.u-net.com
VAT Reg GB 0745 4672 76

invoice to

Trends	
4 Friar Street	
Broadfield	
BR1 3RF	

invoice no	787923
account	3993
your reference	47609
date/tax point	02 10 20-3

deliver to

as above

product code	description	quantity	price	unit	total	discount %	net
45B	Blue toebar socks	100	2.36	pair	236.00	10.00	212.40

terms
Net monthly
Carriage paid
E & OE

goods total	212.40
VAT	37.17
TOTAL	249.57

an invoice with 10% trade discount deducted

settlement (cash) discount

Settlement discount (also known as **cash discount**) is a discount offered by the seller to the buyer to encourage the buyer to settle up straightaway or in a short space of time rather than waiting the thirty or more days specified on the invoice. For example, the terms on the bottom of the invoice may include the phrase:*"Settlement discount of 2.5% for payment within seven days"*. This means that the seller will allow 2.5% off the net invoice price (ie the price before VAT is added on) if the invoice is settled within seven days of the invoice date.

There are two important points to remember:

1   VAT charged on an invoice with settlement (cash) discount offered is calculated on the invoice amount **after** deduction of settlement discount.

2   The invoice total is the sum of this reduced amount of VAT and the goods total **before** deduction of settlement discount.

If we take the Cool Socks invoice on the next page, the calculations for a cash discount of 2.5% are as follows:

Step 1	Calculate the total price before trade discount 100 x £2.36 = £236.00
Step 2	Calculate the trade discount (as before) £236.00 x 10% (ie 10/100) = £23.60
Step 3	Calculate the net price/Goods Total (as before) £236.00 - £23.60 = £212.40
Step 4	NOW calculate the settlement discount £212.40 x 2.5% (ie 2.5/100) = £5.31
Step 5	Calculate the reduced goods total (this is not written on the invoice) £212.40 - £5.31 = £207.09
Step 6	Calculate the VAT on this lower amount £207.09 x 17.5% (ie 17.5/100) = £36.24
Step 7	Calculate the total invoice price (**using the goods total before deduction of settlement discount**) £212.40 + £36.24 = £248.64

INVOICE

COOL SOCKS LIMITED

Unit 45 Elgar Estate, Broadfield, BR7 4ER
Tel 01908 765314 Fax 01908 765951 Email toni@cool.u-net.com
VAT Reg GB 0745 4672 76

invoice to

Trends **4 Friar Street** **Broadfield** **BR1 3RF**	

invoice no	**787923**
account	**3993**
your reference	**47609**
date/tax point	**02 10 20-3**

deliver to

as above

product code	description	quantity	price	unit	total	discount %	net
45B	**Blue toebar socks**	100	2.36	pair	236.00	10.00	212.40

goods total	212.40
VAT	36.24
TOTAL	248.64

terms

2.5% settlement discount for payment within 7 days, otherwise net monthly

Carriage paid

E & OE

an invoice with 10% trade discount deducted and 2.5% settlement discount allowed for quick settlement

VALUE ADDED TAX (VAT) – A 'SALES TAX'

what is Value Added Tax (VAT)?

VAT is a UK sales tax on the selling price charged to buyers.

As we have seen on some of the business documents illustrated in this chapter, VAT is added to the price of items sold after discount has been deducted. VAT is a **sales tax** paid by the consumer and administered and collected for the Government by **HM Revenue & Customs**.

Businesses must keep accurate records of VAT paid and collected. This means filing financial documents such as invoices and credit notes for a minimum period of six years. HM Revenue & Customs tax inspectors visit businesses from time-to-time to ensure that VAT is being charged correctly and that there are no VAT 'fiddles' taking place.

some useful VAT calculations

In your studies you are likely to be asked to carry out a variety of calculations involving VAT. Here are some of the more common ones.

what is the VAT to be charged?

If you need to work out the VAT on a given amount you apply the formula:

$$\text{amount} \times \frac{17.5}{100} \text{ (ie the VAT rate)} = \text{VAT payable}$$

VAT chargeable on £100 is therefore $£100 \times \frac{17.5}{100} = £17.50$

Note that when calculating VAT, the VAT total is always rounded down to the nearest penny; eg VAT of £2.56<u>78</u> becomes £2.5<u>6</u> and not £2.5<u>7</u>.

calculating the VAT when the VAT is included but not shown

If you are given a total amount, for an example a shop till receipt which does not show the VAT amount, you may need to work out both the VAT content and also the amount before VAT is added (the 'VAT exclusive' amount). This is done by using the formula:

$$\frac{\text{VAT percentage} \times \text{amount which includes VAT}}{100 + \text{VAT percentage}} = \text{VAT content}$$

Note that this calculation can also be carried out by multiplying the amount which includes VAT by a fraction known as the 'VAT fraction' which is provided by HM Revenue & Customs. If the VAT rate is is 17.5%, the VAT included can be calculated by multiplying the amount including VAT by $7/47$.

AUTHORISING AND CHECKING INVOICES

credit limits

The credit limit of a customer is the maximum amount which the seller will allow the customer to owe at any one time.

Part of the accounting control system of a business is to set credit limits for its established customers and to establish limits for new customers. Each time that an invoice is issued, a check should be made against the credit limit of that customer.

authorisation of invoices

Most invoices issued will be within the credit limit and processed with the authority of the person in charge of invoicing. What if the credit limit will be exceeded? No business will refuse to supply a good customer. It may be that payment will soon come in from the buyer, or the amount involved is relatively small. In these cases the invoice will need authorisation from a more senior person in the accounts department. It is quite possible that a credit limit may have to be raised if a customer is buying more goods or services, and, of course, is paying invoices on time.

the need to check invoices

Few things are more annoying to a buyer than an incorrect invoice – the wrong goods, the wrong price, the wrong discount, and so on. It wastes the buyer's time and may require an adjusting credit note to be issued. It is essential that a number of important details are checked by the accounts staff of the seller before invoices are authorised and sent out.

What resources will the person checking need? He/she will need to look at:

- the purchase order relating to the invoice (this is very important)
- the seller's own record of any price quoted (eg a printed catalogue or a product database)
- the seller's file record of the buyer (either paper-based or on the computer) which should give the credit limit and the discount allowed

the checks to be made

- Is the **correct customer** being invoiced? There are often customers with similar names; the customer coding must be carefully checked.
- Are the goods being sent to the **correct place**? Sometimes the delivery address can be different from the address normally held on file.

- Are the **correct goods** being sent? The product coding on the purchase order must be checked carefully against the description; it is possible that the buyer has quoted an incorrect code
- Is the **quantity** correct?
- Is the **unit** correct? Is it a box of products or an individual item being requested?
- Is the **price** correct?
- Is the **correct discount** percentage being allowed to the customer? Do any special terms apply? The list of discounts or customer file will need to be looked at.
- Are the **calculations** on the invoice correct? This is very important if the invoice has not been produced on a computer. The normal checks for a straightforward invoice with trade discount deducted are:

    quantity x unit price = total before discount

    total before discount x discount % = discount

    total before discount – discount = net total

    net total x VAT % = VAT

    net total + VAT = invoice total

If the invoice is for more than one one product, all the invoice 'lines' must be carefully and individually checked and the addition also checked.

Very important note:

If there is **settlement discount** being offered, the VAT amount must be calculated on the net total after deduction of settlement discount, but the invoice total must assume that discount is not being taken and so equals:

    net total before deduction of settlement discount plus VAT amount calculated on net total after deduction of settlement discount

This does not sound completely logical, but it is correct!

DEALING WITH DISCREPANCIES

Discrepancies on financial documents can occur in the following situations:

- **The discrepancy is found in the internal checking process**, before the document is issued. In this case the document will have to be passed back to the person or section which made the mistake and a new corrected document will have to be issued and authorised; normally the original document reference number can be retained
- **The buyer finds the discrepancy after the document has been issued.** In this case an apology will have to be made by the seller to the buyer and a correcting document issued; under no circumstances should the buyer alter or correct the document

FILING – RETENTION OF DOCUMENTS

coding systems

It is important in any business that documents can be found and referred to easily, either in paper format, or on a computer system.

Filing systems are normally organised using either an **alphabetic** or a **numeric** coding system:

- customer files are normally filed alphabetically by name
- invoices are normally filed numerically by invoice number

Sometimes coding may be **alpha-numeric**, using a mixture of letters and numbers. For example customers who have 'JON' as the first three letters of their name – 'Jones' for example – may be coded JON010, JON011, JON012, and so on.

filing retention policy

Over the years businesses are likely to accumulate a large volume of:

- paper-based documents: financial documents, letters, contracts
- electronically based data: emails, database files, spreadsheet files

The question then arises: "How long should we keep all these records for?" The answer is that businesses often have a **retention policy** stating that records are normally kept for **six years, plus the current year**.

The reasons for this are legal requirements. Legislation covering company law, taxation and data protection generally requires that records should be kept for anywhere between three and six years.

Another legal reason is that **after six years** if anyone wants to take legal action against a business, they are prevented from doing so by a principle known as **limitation of action**. That is why all necessary evidence is kept for six years.

destruction of filing records

A business should always keep its filing records securely so that people who are not authorised to access the records are prevented from getting hold of confidential information. After the six years has elapsed the records can be destroyed or shredded (paper records), or 'wiped' (data held electronically). This includes the wiping or destruction of a computer's hard disk if a computer is being replaced.

■ When a business sells goods or services on credit it will deal with a number of financial documents. The most important of these are the
- purchase order
- delivery note
- invoice
- credit note
- statement

■ The seller of the goods or services requests payment by means of an invoice and then reminds the buyer by means of a regular statement of account (normally monthly).

■ Discounts – reductions in the selling price – are often given by the seller to the buyer. These include trade discount, bulk discount and settlement discount for early payment. Trade and bulk discounts are deducted by the seller from the invoice total. Settlement discount is deducted by the buyer.

■ A refund due to the buyer will be acknowledged and documented by means of a credit note.

■ All documents are normally coded (given a numeric or alpha-numeric code) for reference purposes.

■ VAT (Value Added Tax), a sales tax payable on most goods and services, is included on the majority of invoices and credit notes.

■ All documents should be checked carefully by the seller to make sure that the right goods or services have been supplied, and at the right price. It is essential that items such as discounts, VAT and totals are calculated correctly.

■ Financial documents will need to be authorised before they are sent out.

■ Any discrepancies found on the documents either by the seller or the buyer should be dealt with promptly.

■ Documents are normally filed away for reference purposes. The documents will be coded for easy access and retained for at least six years.

purchase order	a document issued by the buyer of goods and services, sent to the seller, indicating the goods or services required
delivery note	a document sent by the seller to the buyer with the goods, detailing what has been sent
invoice	a document issued by the seller of goods or services indicating the amount owing and the required payment date
credit note	a document issued by the seller of the goods or services reducing the amount owed by the buyer
statement	a document issued by the seller to the buyer summarising invoices, credit notes issued and payments received and stating the amount owed
trade discount	a percentage reduction in the selling price given by the seller to the buyer because of the trading relationship
bulk discount	a discount given by the seller to the buyer for bulk purchases, ie purchases over certain quantities or over certain money amounts
settlement (cash) discount	a percentage reduction in the selling price given to the buyer if the buyer pays within a specified short space of time
Value Added Tax (VAT)	a government tax on sales, normally calculated on invoices and credit notes
credit limit	the maximum amount the seller will allow the customer to owe at any one time
coding	document references using numeric, alphabetic or alpha-numeric identification systems
document retention policy	the requirement for an organisation to keep documents for a specified minimum period of time, normally six years plus the current year

Activities

2.1 What type of financial document would normally be used when goods are sold on credit:

(a)   to be sent with the goods from the seller to the buyer, and listing the goods sent?

(b)   as a formal notification of the amount owed?

(c)   to remind the buyer of the amount owed to the seller?

(d)   as a formal notification from the seller of a refund made to the buyer?

(e)   to order the goods from the seller in the first place?

2.2 (a)   Explain the term 'trade discount'.

(b)   You supply goods priced at £159.50 to a customer at a trade discount of 30%. What would the total invoice amount be, assuming a VAT rate of 17.5% and no further discounts?

2.3 Compuworld sells blank CDs and has a special sales offer. A box of ten formatted disks normally sells at £8.00 (excluding VAT). Compuworld is offering to give a 20% bulk discount for orders of ten boxes or more. One morning it receives the following orders:

(a)   20 boxes ordered by Osborne Electronics Limited

(b)   50 boxes ordered by Helfield College

(c)   5 boxes ordered by Jim Masters

(d)   1,000 boxes ordered by Trigger Trading Limited

Calculate in each case

- the total cost before discount

- the discount

- the cost after discount

- the VAT at the current rate

- the total cost

2.4 Recalculate the totals in Activity 2.3 allowing for a settlement (cash) discount of 2.5%.

2.5 You work as one of three assistants in an accounts office. Your supervisor is off sick. You receive an urgent and large purchase order from a customer and find that the product code and goods description do not match up. The goods have to be despatched on the same day. What is the problem and what would you do about it?

2.6 (a)   Give three examples of coding found on financial documents prepared by a seller.

(b)   Explain why coding is important.

2.7 Invoices filed by a business are normally retained for at least

(a) one year plus the current year

(b) six years plus the current year

(c) ten years plus the current year

(d) twenty years plus the current year

Which of these options is correct?

2.8 • Check the invoice extracts shown below.

• State what is wrong with them.

• Calculate the correct final totals.

Note: VAT is always rounded down to the nearest penny.

invoice (a)

description	quantity	price	total	discount %	net
Cotton shirts (red)	10	9.50	95.00	20	85.50

goods total	85.50
VAT @ 17.5%	14.96
TOTAL	100.45

invoice (b)

description	quantity	price	total	discount %	net
'Crazy Surfin' T-shirts (yellow)	50	5.00	225.00	10	202.50

goods total	202.50
VAT @ 17.5%	35.44
TOTAL	237.94

2.9 You work in the Accounts Department of Pool Cleaning Services Limited, a business which maintains swimming pools, spa baths and jacuzzis.

It is 31 July 20-3 and you are looking through the file for the account of Mr Henry Simpson. Your file shows that you issued an invoice on 8 July (shown below) and a credit note on 14 July for a 10% trade discount which should have been deducted from the invoice (see next page).

You also note from last month's statement that Mr Simpson still owed you £58.75 on 1 July for a call out charge he had not yet paid. You received a cheque for this amount on 4 July.

You are to prepare a statement for Mr H Simpson as at 31 July 20-3. It should show opening and closing balances and transactions for the month. A blank statement is shown on the next page.

INVOICE

Pool Cleaning Services Limited

Unit 5 Neptune Estate, Mereford, MR7 4EF
Tel 01908 352456 Fax 01908 352466 Email mail@poolcleaning-services.com
VAT Reg GB 0745 4872 21

invoice to

H Simpson 45 Bishops Avenue Marston Hackett MR7 9JH	

invoice no	**10982**
account	**234**
your reference	**verbal**
date/tax point	**08 07 20-3**

description	total	discount %	net
Annual swimming pool service, 27 June 20-3	290.00	0.00	290.00

Net Total	290.00
VAT	50.75
TOTAL	340.75

terms
Net monthly

extract from credit note No. 2378 dated 14 July

description		total	discount	net
Annual swimming pool service		29.00	0.00	29.00

Reason for credit
10% discount allowable on invoice
10982

NET TOTAL	29.00
VAT	5.07
TOTAL	34.07

STATEMENT OF ACCOUNT

Pool Cleaning Services Limited

Unit 5 Neptune Estate, Mereford, MR7 4EF
Tel 01908 352456 Fax 01908 352466 Email mail@poolcleaning-services.com
VAT Reg GB 0745 4872 21

TO

account

date

date	details	debit £	credit £	balance £

	TOTAL	£

3 Accounting for sales and sales returns

this chapter covers...

This chapter focuses on using the accounting system to record the details of sales and sales returns.

Having looked in the previous chapter at the documents and procedures involved in selling on credit we will now take the financial documents of sales invoices and credit notes for sales and record them in books of prime entry (day books) and in the book-keeping system of general ledger and sales ledger.

We will be using two books of prime entry:

- sales day book
- sales returns day book

Information from these day books will then be transferred into the book-keeping system using accounts in general ledger and sales ledger.

The chapter also covers the methods of coding, used to trace transactions through the accounting system

Note:

In this chapter we use the International Accounting Standards term 'receivable' to mean a person who owes money to a business; normally this is a customer. You may also in your studies and assessments come across the traditional term 'debtor' which means exactly the same thing.

THE ACCOUNTING SYSTEM

We have seen earlier in Chapter 1 (page 4) that the accounting system comprises a number of stages of recording and presenting financial transactions:

- financial documents
- books of prime entry (eg day books)
- double-entry book-keeping
- trial balance

In this chapter we look at how financial documents for credit sales and sales returns transactions are recorded in the books of prime entry, together with the entries to be made in the double-entry book-keeping accounts. Later in the book we will see how a list of the balances of the double-entry accounts is used to form the trial balance (Chapter 11).

ACCOUNTING FOR CREDIT SALES AND SALES RETURNS

In this chapter we focus on credit sales and sales returns transactions. Cash sales transactions will be seen when we study the cash book (Chapter 8).

In accounting, the term 'sales' means: **the sale of goods in which the business trades**.

This means that an office stationery shop will record as sales things such as photocopier paper, ring binders, etc – the income from the goods in which the business trades is described as **revenue income**. By contrast, if the shop sells off its old cash till when it is replaced with a new one, this is not recorded as sales but, instead, is accounted for as the sale of an asset – such income is described as **capital income**.

'Sales returns' are when goods previously sold on credit are returned to the business by its customers.

The diagram on the next page shows the order in which the accounting records are prepared for credit sales and sales returns transactions. You will see that the steps are:

- start with a **financial document**, either a sales invoice or a credit note issued
- enter it in the appropriate **book of prime entry** (the first accounting book in which the financial document is recorded and summarised), either sales day book or sales returns day book

- transfer the information from the book of prime entry into the double-entry accounts in the **general ledger**
- transfer the information from the book of prime entry into the accounts of receivables(debtors) – ie the customers – in the **sales ledger**

accounting for credit sales and sales returns

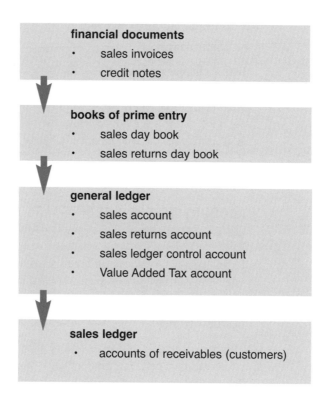

financial documents
- sales invoices
- credit notes

books of prime entry
- sales day book
- sales returns day book

general ledger
- sales account
- sales returns account
- sales ledger control account
- Value Added Tax account

sales ledger
- accounts of receivables (customers)

We will now look in more detail at the mechanics of the books of prime entry and the double-entry book-keeping system. We shall then apply the accounting system to the recording of credit sales and sales returns.

BOOKS OF PRIME ENTRY

The books of prime entry include a number of **day books** which list money amounts and other details taken from financial documents.

The day books used for credit sales and sales returns are:
- sales day book
- sales returns day book

These are called books of prime entry because they are the first place in the accounting system where financial documents are recorded. Note that books of prime entry are not part of double-entry book-keeping, but are used to give totals which are then entered into the accounts.

The reasons for using books of prime entry are:

- the totals from the books of prime entry can be checked before they are entered into the ledger accounts
- the use of books of prime entry for a large number of regular transactions, such as sales, means that there are fewer transactions to enter into the double-entry accounts
- the work of the accounts department can be divided up – one person can enter transactions in the books of prime entry, while another can concentrate on the double-entry accounts

A sales day book is written up as shown below, with sample entries which will have been taken from individual sales invoices:

	Sales Day Book					SDB21
Date	Details	Invoice number	Reference	Total	VAT*	Net
20-4				£	£	£
5 Jan	Doyle & Co Ltd	901	SL058	141	21	120
8 Jan	Sparkes & Sons Ltd	902	SL127	188	28	160
13 Jan	T Young	903	SL179	94	14	80
15 Jan	A-Z Supplies Ltd	904	SL003	235	35	200
21 Jan	Sparkes & Sons Ltd	905	SL127	141	21	120
31 Jan	Totals for month			799	119	680
				GL1200	GL2200	GL4100

* VAT = 17.5 per cent

Notes:

- Sales day book is prepared from financial documents – sales invoices issued to customers.
- The code 'SDB21' at the top of the day book is used for cross-referencing to the book-keeping system: here it indicates that this is page 21 of the sales day book (SDB).
- The **reference** column (also known as the folio column) cross-references here to 'SL' – the Sales Ledger – followed by the account number of the receivable (customer).

- The **total** column records the amount of each financial document, ie after VAT has been included.
- The code 'GL' beneath the totals amounts refers to the account numbers in the General Ledger.
- Sales day book is totalled at appropriate intervals – daily, weekly, or monthly (as here) – and the total of the **net** column tells the business the amount of credit sales for the period.
- The amounts from sales day book are recorded in the ledger accounts.

a note on day books and Value Added Tax

When a business is VAT-registered, VAT is charged on invoices and credit notes issued to customers. When writing up day books from VAT invoices and credit notes:

- enter the total amount of the invoice or credit note into the 'total' column
- enter the VAT amount in the VAT column
- enter the net amount of the invoice or credit note, before VAT is added, in the 'net' column

Later in this chapter we shall see how the VAT columns from the sales and sales returns day books are entered into the double-entry accounts.

WRITING UP THE SALES DAY BOOK

The sales day book lists the credit sales made by a business. Following the issue of an invoice for each transaction, the sales day book is prepared from sales invoices, as seen on the previous page. In order to write up the sales day book, we take the sales invoices that have been checked and authorised and enter the details:

- date of invoice
- name of customer
- sales invoice number
- cross reference to the customer's account number in the sales ledger, eg 'SL058'
- enter the total amount of the invoice into the total column
- enter the VAT amount shown on the invoice
- enter the net amount of the invoice (often described as 'goods or services total'), before VAT is added

The next step in the accounting process is to make entries in the double-entry accounts. The underlying theory and principles of this process are described on the pages that follow.

DOUBLE-ENTRY SYSTEM

The accounting system is organised on the basis of a number of **accounts** which record the money amounts of financial transactions: collectively these accounts are known as 'the ledger'.

Accounts are kept in the names of customers and of suppliers of the business, and also for other transactions such as the receipt and payment of money for various purposes. Accounts can be kept in the form of:

- handwritten records
- computer records

In a handwritten system, accounts are maintained either in a bound book or a series of separate sheets of paper or card – each account occupying a separate page. The business can set up its own manual system, or can buy one ready-made from a business supplies shop.

In a computerised system each account is held as data in a computer file. Whether a handwritten or computerised system is being used, the principles remain the same. For the moment we will concentrate on handwritten accounts.

A handwritten system can either use specially ruled accounting paper – known as ledger paper – which can be purchased from a business supplies shop, or a suitable layout can be set up as follows:

Debit			**Name of Account, eg Sales Account**		Credit
Date	Details	£	Date	Details	£
↑ of transaction	↑ name of other account	↑ amount of transaction			

Note the following points about the layout of this account:

- the name of the account is written at the top (often followed by the account number)
- the account is divided into two identical halves, separated by a central double vertical line
- the left-hand side is called the 'debit' (or 'Dr') side
- the right-hand side is called the 'credit' (or 'Cr') side
- the date, details and amount of the transaction are entered in the account
- in the 'details' column is entered the name of the other account (or book of prime entry) involved – this acts as a cross reference; also, a 'reference' column (not illustrated here) is often incorporated on each side of an account – to the left of the money amount columns

In practice, each account would occupy a whole page in a handwritten system but, to save space when doing exercises, it is usual to put several accounts on a page. In future, in this book, the account layout will be simplified as follows to make the process clearer:

Dr		Sales Account		Cr
20-4	£	20-4		£
		31 Jan Sales Day Book SDB21		680

This layout is often known in accounting jargon as a **'T' account**; it is used to illustrate accounts because it separates in a simple way the two sides – debit and credit – of the account. An alternative style of account has three money columns: debit, credit and balance. This type of account is commonly used for bank statements and computer accounting statements. Because the balance of the account is calculated after every transaction, it is known as a 'running balance account.'

debits and credits

The principle of double-entry book-keeping is that two entries are made, for each financial transaction, usually in different accounts:

- one account is **debited** with the money amount of the transaction, and
- one account is **credited** with the money amount of the transaction

The principle is often known as the **dual aspect** of book-keeping, ie each transaction has a dual effect on the accounts – one account gains by recording a receipt or an asset, while another account gives value by recording a payment or a liability.

Debit entries are on the left-hand side of the appropriate account, while credit entries are on the right. The rules for debits and credits are:

- **debit entry** – the account which gains value, or records an asset, or an expense
- **credit entry** – the account which gives value, or records a liability, or an income item

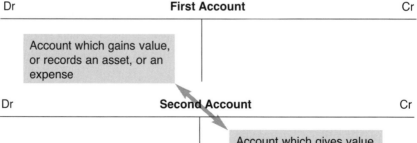

Dr	First Account	Cr
Account which gains value, or records an asset, or an expense		

Dr	Second Account	Cr
		Account which gives value, or records a liability, or an income item

When one entry has been identified as a debit or credit, the other entry will be on the opposite side of the other account.

DIVISION OF THE LEDGER

Accounts are normally written on separate pages of a book known as 'the ledger'. In practice, several separate ledgers are kept: for credit sales transactions we shall be making use of the following ledgers:

- **general ledger** (also often referred to as the nominal ledger) containing sales account, sales returns account, sales ledger control account, Value Added Tax account, together with other accounts kept by the business

- **sales ledger**, which is a subsidiary ledger to general ledger, and contains the accounts of the firm's receivables

The diagram shown below illustrates the way in which ledgers and accounts are used in connection with sales:

GENERAL LEDGER	SALES LEDGER
• **sales account** – to record sales invoices issued	a subsidiary ledger containing the separate 'memorandum' accounts for each **receivable**, ie customers who owe money to the business
• **sales returns account** – to record credit notes issued	
• **sales ledger control account** – to record the total amount of receivables	
• **Value Added Tax account** – to record the VAT amounts of credit sales and sales returns	

Notes:

- **General ledger** also contains a number of other accounts, for example accounts for items such as purchases, expenses, receipts and payments, and also the assets and liabilities of the business.

- **Sales ledger** is a subsidiary ledger to general ledger because it gives a detailed breakdown of the amount of the sales ledger control account in general ledger. It does this by showing the separate accounts for each receivable of the business: these accounts are called **memorandum accounts** because they provide a record of individual amounts owed by each receivable. The total of these accounts should always equal the balance (total amount) of the sales ledger control account.

ACCOUNTING SYSTEM FOR CREDIT SALES

The accounting system for credit sales fits together in the following way:

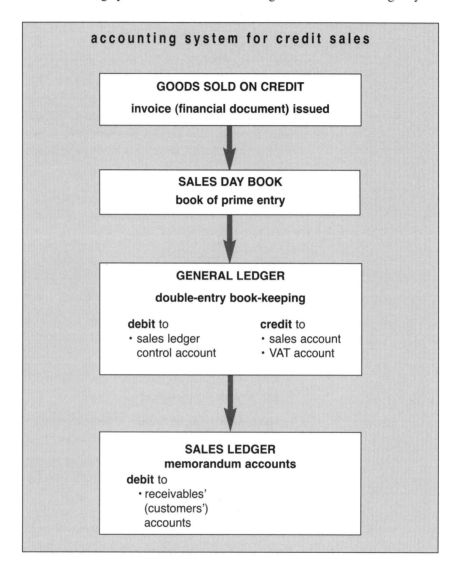

We will now look in more detail at the sales day book and the accounting system for credit sales.

In the examples which follow we will assume that the business is registered for Value Added Tax, and therefore VAT is charged on invoices issued to customers.

The VAT rate used in the examples is 17.5%.

BOOK-KEEPING FOR CREDIT SALES

After the sales day book has been written up and totalled, the information from it is transferred to the double-entry system in the general ledger.

The completed sales day book is shown below, followed by the accounts in the general ledger which record the credit sales transactions listed in the sales day book.

Sales Day Book						SDB21
Date	Details	Invoice number	Reference	Total	VAT	Net
20-4				£	£	£
5 Jan	Doyle & Co Ltd	901	SL058	141	21	120
8 Jan	Sparkes & Sons Ltd	902	SL127	188	28	160
13 Jan	T Young	903	SL179	94	14	80
15 Jan	A-Z Supplies Ltd	904	SL003	235	35	200
21 Jan	Sparkes & Sons Ltd	905	SL127	141	21	120
31 Jan	Totals for month			799	119	680
				GL1200	GL2200	GL4100

GENERAL LEDGER

Dr		**Sales Ledger Control Account** (GL1200)		Cr
20-4	£	20-4		£
31 Jan Sales Day Book SDB21 799				

Dr		**Value Added Tax Account** (GL2200)		Cr
20-4	£	20-4		£
		31 Jan Sales Day Book SDB21	119	

Dr		**Sales Account** (GL4100)		Cr
20-4	£	20-4		£
		31 Jan Sales Day Book SDB21	680	

Note that from the sales day book on the previous page:

- the total of the total column, £799, has been debited to sales ledger control account (which records the asset of receivables)

- the total of the VAT column, £119, has been credited to VAT account (which has given value)

- the total of the net column, £680, has been credited to sales account (which has given value)

- each entry in the general ledger is cross-referenced back to the page number of the sales day book; here the reference is 'SDB21'.

The last step is to record the amount of sales made to each receivable. We do this by recording the sales invoices in the sales ledger as follows:

SALES LEDGER

Dr			**A-Z Supplies Ltd** (SL003)	Cr	
20-4		£	20-4		£
15 Jan	Sales SDB21	235			

Dr			**Doyle & Co Ltd** (SL058)	Cr	
20-4		£	20-4		£
5 Jan	Sales SDB21	141			

Dr			**Sparkes & Sons Ltd** (SL127)	Cr	
20-4		£	20-4		£
8 Jan	Sales SDB21	188			
21 Jan	Sales SDB21	141			

Dr			**T Young** (SL179)	Cr	
20-4		£	20-4		£
13 Jan	Sales SDB21	94			

Notes:

- the sales day book (see page 49) incorporates a reference column, used to cross-reference each transaction to the personal account of each receivable in the sales ledger (SL); this enables a particular transaction to be traced from financial document (invoice issued), through the book of prime entry (sales day book), to the receivable's account

- each entry in the sales ledger is cross-referenced back to the page number of the sales day book; here the reference is 'SDB21'.

memorandum accounts

The accounts in sales ledger are prepared following the principles of double-entry book-keeping. However, they are **memorandum accounts,** which means they are used to provide a note of how much each receivable owes to the business.

As such they are not part of double-entry but are represented in the general ledger by sales ledger control account. This means that, here, the £799 debit entry is split up in the sales ledger between the four receivables' memorandum accounts. Note that memorandum accounts are often referred to as **subsidiary accounts**.

ACCOUNTING SYSTEM FOR SALES RETURNS

Sales returns (or returns in) are when goods previously sold on credit are returned to the business by its customers. A credit note (see page 24) is the financial document issued by a business when it makes a refund to a customer who has bought goods on credit. A credit note reduces the amount owed by the receivable.

The accounting procedures for sales returns involve:

- **financial documents** – credit notes issued to customers
- **book of prime entry** – sales returns day book
- **double-entry accounts** – general ledger (sales returns account, which records the total net amount of credit notes issued, Value Added Tax account, which records the VAT amount of sales returns, and sales ledger control account, which records the asset of receivables)
- **sales ledger** – the memorandum accounts for each individual receivable of the business

The accounting system for sales returns is shown in the diagram on the next page.

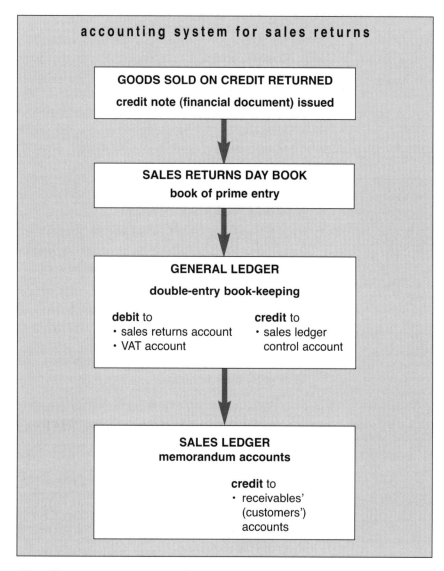

We will now look in more detail at the sales returns day book and the double-entry accounts for sales returns. Note that the business is registered for Value Added Tax.

SALES RETURNS DAY BOOK

The sales returns day book uses virtually the same layout as the sales day book seen on page 49 of this chapter. It operates in a similar way, storing up information about sales returns transactions until such time as a transfer is made into the double-entry accounts system. The prime documents for sales returns day book are credit notes issued to customers.

The sales returns day book is written up as follows, with sample entries:

Sales Returns Day Book						SRDB5
Date	Details	Credit note no	Reference	Total	VAT*	Net
20-4				£	£	£
15 Jan	T Young	702	SL179	47	7	40
27 Jan	A-Z Supplies Ltd	703	SL003	141	21	120
31 Jan	Totals for month			188	28	160
				GL1200	GL2200	GL4110

* VAT = 17.5 per cent

Notes:

- The sales returns day book is prepared from credit notes (or copies of credit notes) issued to customers.

- The day book is totalled at appropriate intervals – weekly or monthly.

- The VAT-inclusive amounts from the total column are credited to the receivables' individual 'memorandum' accounts in sales ledger.

- The total of the VAT column is transferred to the debit of the VAT account in general ledger.

- The total of the net column tells the business the amount of sales returns for the period. This amount is transferred to the debit of sales returns account in general ledger.

- The total column records the amount of each credit note issued, ie after VAT has been included. This amount is transferred to the credit of sales ledger control account in general ledger.

BOOK-KEEPING FOR SALES RETURNS

After the sales returns day book has been written up and totalled, the information from it is transferred into the double-entry system.

The accounts in the general ledger to record the transactions from the above sales returns day book (including any other transactions already recorded on these accounts) are as follows (see next page):

GENERAL LEDGER

Dr	Sales Ledger Control Account (GL1200)		Cr
20-4	£	20-4	£
31 Jan Sales Day Book SDB21 799		31 Jan Sales Returns	
		Day Book SRDB5	188

Dr	Value Added Tax Account (GL2200)		Cr
20-4	£	20-4	£
31 Jan Sales Returns		31 Jan Sales Day Book SDB21	119
Day Book SRDB5	28		

Dr	Sales Returns Account (GL4110)		Cr
20-4	£	20-4	£
31 Jan Sales Returns			
Day Book SRDB5	160		

The last step is to record the amount of sales returns from each receivable. We do this by recording the sales returns in the memorandum accounts for each receivable in the sales ledger as follows:

SALES LEDGER

Dr	A-Z Supplies Ltd (SL003)		Cr
20-4	£	20-4	£
15 Jan Sales SDB21	235	27 Jan Sales Returns SRDB5	141

Dr	T Young (SL179)		Cr
20-4	£	20-4	£
12 Jan Sales SDB21	94	15 Jan Sales Returns SRDB5	47

THE USE OF ANALYSED SALES DAY BOOKS

As well as the layout of the day books we have seen so far in this chapter, a business can use analysed day books whenever it needs to analyse its sales and sales returns between:

- different departments, eg a store with departments for furniture, carpets and curtains, hardware
- different categories of goods sold, eg paint, wallpaper, brushes, or services supplied

For example, a wholesaler of decorators' supplies may decide to write up its sales day book as shown below.

Sales Day Book									SDB48
Date	Details	Invoice no	Reference	Total	VAT*	Net	Paint	Wallpaper	Brushes
20-4				£	£	£	£	£	£
9 Aug	DIY Sales Limited	1478	SL059	235	35	200	75	125	–
12 Aug	T Lane Decorators	1479	SL108	141	21	120	–	100	20
16 Aug	Colour Painters Limited	1480	SL038	329	49	280	150	100	30
23 Aug	Southern Decorators	1481	SL211	188	28	160	100	60	–
31 Aug	Totals for month			893	133	760	325	385	50
				GL1200	GL2200		GL4150	GL4160	GL4170

* VAT = 17.5 per cent

Analysed sales day books and sales returns day books can be adapted to suit the particular needs of a business. Thus, there is not a standard way in which to present the books of prime entry – the needs of the user of the information are all important. By using analysed day books, the owner of the business can see how much has been sold by departments, or categories of goods and services.

Notes:

- The reference column is to 'SL' (Sales Ledger) and the customer's account number.
- The code 'GL' beneath the totals amounts refers to the account numbers in General Ledger.
- The analysis columns – here paint, wallpaper, brushes – show the amount of sales net of VAT (ie before VAT is added).
- The analysis columns analyse the net amount – by products sold or services supplied – from sales invoices.

METHODS OF CODING IN ACCOUNTING SYSTEMS

As a business grows, methods of coding need to be used to trace transactions through the accounting system, ie through financial documents, books of prime entry, double-entry book-keeping and the trial balance. There are a number of different systems of coding in use:

- **alphabetical**, where letters are used, eg 'ABC'
- **numeric**, where numbers are used, eg '123'
- **alpha-numeric**, where both letters and numbers are used, eg 'ABC123'

Uses of coding in the stages of the accounting system are:

financial documents

- each document, eg invoice, credit note, is numbered
- goods listed on invoices have reference number or letters, eg catalogue reference, which, if a computer accounting system is used, will enable the business to analyse sales by product

books of prime entry

- each page of the day books is numbered
- the number of the document, eg invoice, credit note is recorded
- the code of the debtors or creditors account is recorded, eg 'SL' for sales ledger, followed by the account number or short name (see below)

ledger accounts

- the accounts system is divided into sections: general ledger, sales ledger, and purchases ledger
- general ledger accounts are numbered and are often arranged in a particular order, for example

0100 – 1399	Assets
2100 – 2399	Liabilities
3100 – 3399	Capital
4100 – 4399	Sales
5100 – 5399	Purchases
6100 – 6399	Expenses

- each account in the sales ledger is numbered eg 'SL058' (or some accounting systems use an abbreviated name, or short name, eg the account of Peterhead Trading Company might be coded as 'PETER')

We will now summarise what we have covered in this chapter by means of a Case Study which shows how the accounting system works for credit sales and sales returns.

Case Study

1.850

1.600

WYVERN TRADERS – CREDIT SALES AND RETURNS

To bring together the material covered in this chapter, we will look at a comprehensive Case Study which makes use of:

- **books of prime entry**
  - sales day book
  - sales returns day book
- **general ledger accounts**
  - sales account
  - sales ledger control account
  - Value Added Tax account
- **sales ledger accounts**
  - receivables' memorandum accounts

The Chapter Summary (pages 60 and 61) also includes diagrams which summarise the procedures for recording credit sales and sales returns transactions in the accounting system.

situation

Wyvern Traders is a wholesaler of stationery and office equipment. The business is registered for VAT. The following are the credit sales and sales returns transactions for April 20-4:

20-4	
2 Apr	Sold goods to P Woodhouse, £200 + VAT, invoice no 2416
9 Apr	P Woodhouse returns goods, £80 + VAT, we issue credit note no 12
14 Apr	Sold goods to Blackheath Limited, £80 + VAT, invoice no 2417
21 Apr	Blackheath Limited returns goods, £40 + VAT, we issue credit note no 13
26 Apr	Sold goods to P Woodhouse, £160 + VAT, invoice no 2418

The day books, general ledger and sales ledger accounts are illustrated on the next two pages: arrows indicate the transfers from the day books to the individual accounts. Note that some accounts have been repeated on both pages in order to show, on the same page, the accounts relating to a particular day book: in practice a business would keep all the transactions together in one account.

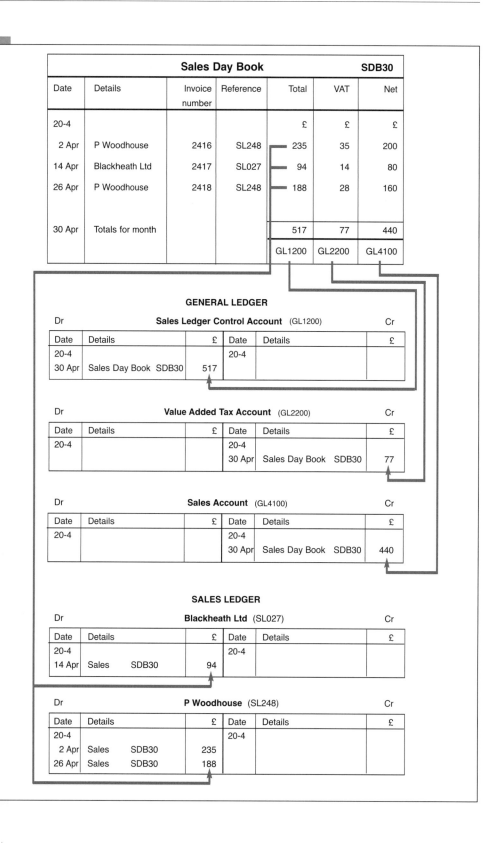

Sales Day Book   SDB30

Date	Details	Invoice number	Reference	Total	VAT	Net
20-4				£	£	£
2 Apr	P Woodhouse	2416	SL248	235	35	200
14 Apr	Blackheath Ltd	2417	SL027	94	14	80
26 Apr	P Woodhouse	2418	SL248	188	28	160
30 Apr	Totals for month			517	77	440
				GL1200	GL2200	GL4100

GENERAL LEDGER

Dr   **Sales Ledger Control Account** (GL1200)   Cr

Date	Details	£	Date	Details	£
20-4			20-4		
30 Apr	Sales Day Book SDB30	517			

Dr   **Value Added Tax Account** (GL2200)   Cr

Date	Details	£	Date	Details	£
20-4			20-4		
			30 Apr	Sales Day Book SDB30	77

Dr   **Sales Account** (GL4100)   Cr

Date	Details	£	Date	Details	£
20-4			20-4		
			30 Apr	Sales Day Book SDB30	440

SALES LEDGER

Dr   **Blackheath Ltd** (SL027)   Cr

Date	Details	£	Date	Details	£
20-4			20-4		
14 Apr	Sales SDB30	94			

Dr   **P Woodhouse** (SL248)   Cr

Date	Details	£	Date	Details	£
20-4			20-4		
2 Apr	Sales SDB30	235			
26 Apr	Sales SDB30	188			

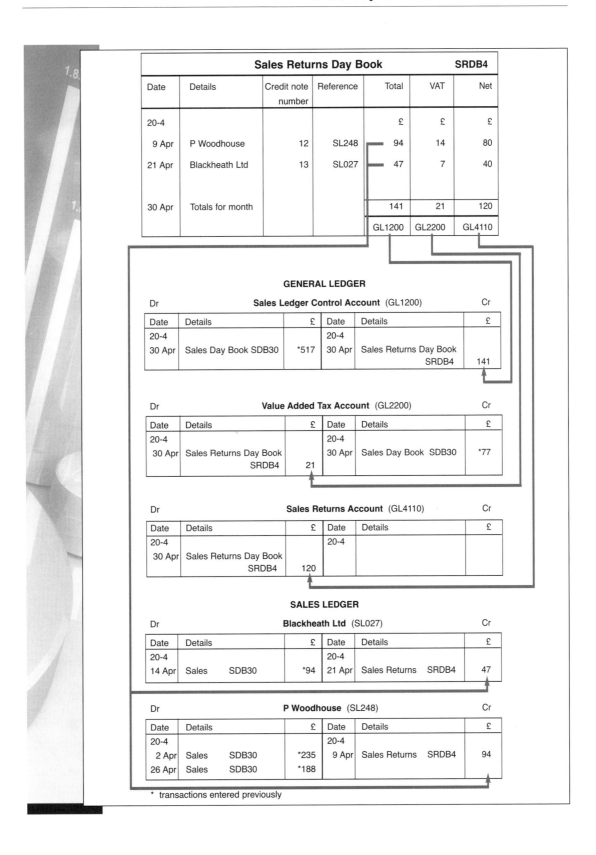

Sales Returns Day Book SRDB4

Date	Details	Credit note number	Reference	Total	VAT	Net
20-4				£	£	£
9 Apr	P Woodhouse	12	SL248	94	14	80
21 Apr	Blackheath Ltd	13	SL027	47	7	40
30 Apr	Totals for month			141	21	120
				GL1200	GL2200	GL4110

GENERAL LEDGER

Dr **Sales Ledger Control Account** (GL1200) Cr

Date	Details	£	Date	Details	£
20-4			20-4		
30 Apr	Sales Day Book SDB30	*517	30 Apr	Sales Returns Day Book SRDB4	141

Dr **Value Added Tax Account** (GL2200) Cr

Date	Details	£	Date	Details	£
20-4			20-4		
30 Apr	Sales Returns Day Book SRDB4	21	30 Apr	Sales Day Book SDB30	*77

Dr **Sales Returns Account** (GL4110) Cr

Date	Details	£	Date	Details	£
20-4			20-4		
30 Apr	Sales Returns Day Book SRDB4	120			

SALES LEDGER

Dr **Blackheath Ltd** (SL027) Cr

Date	Details	£	Date	Details	£
20-4			20-4		
14 Apr	Sales SDB30	*94	21 Apr	Sales Returns SRDB4	47

Dr **P Woodhouse** (SL248) Cr

Date	Details	£	Date	Details	£
20-4			20-4		
2 Apr	Sales SDB30	*235	9 Apr	Sales Returns SRDB4	94
26 Apr	Sales SDB30	*188			

* transactions entered previously

Chapter
Summary

The diagrams below and on the next page summarise the material we have studied so far in this chapter. They show the procedures for recording transactions in the accounting system for credit sales and sales returns.

Further chapter summary points follow on page 62.

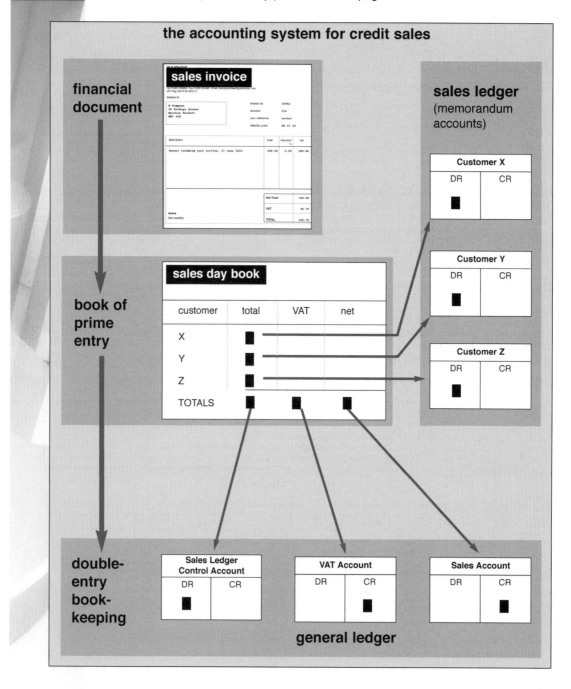

Chapter
Summary

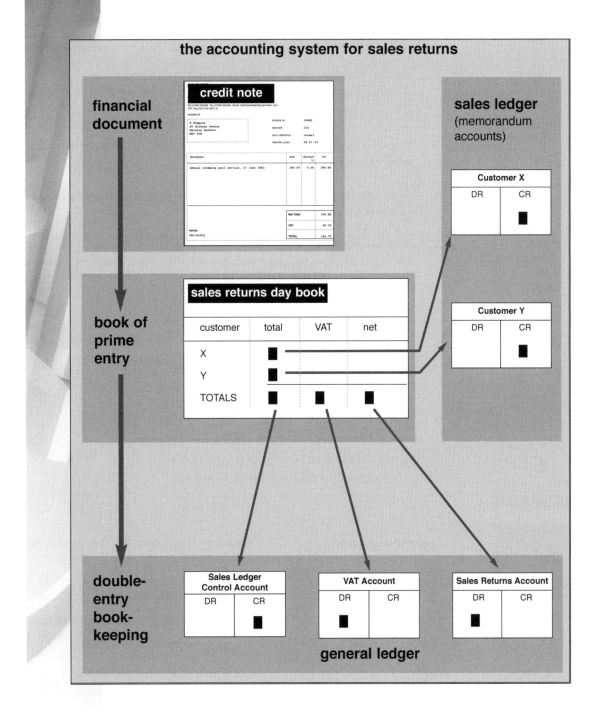

the accounting system for sales returns

financial document

credit note

book of prime entry

sales returns day book

customer	total	VAT	net
X			
Y			
TOTALS			

sales ledger
(memorandum accounts)

Customer X

DR	CR

Customer Y

DR	CR

double-entry book-keeping

Sales Ledger Control Account

DR	CR

VAT Account

DR	CR

Sales Returns Account

DR	CR

general ledger

■ The accounting system comprises a number of specific stages of recording and presenting financial transactions:
  - financial documents
  - books of prime entry (eg day books)
  - double-entry book-keeping
  - trial balance

■ The financial documents relating to credit sales are:
  - sales invoices
  - credit notes issued

■ Sales day book is the book of prime entry for credit sales. It is prepared from sales invoices sent to customers.

■ Sales returns day book is the book of prime entry for sales returns. It is prepared from credit notes issued to customers.

■ Analysed sales and sales returns day books are used when a business wishes to analyse its sales between different departments or different categories of goods sold or services supplied.

■ Recording credit sales in the double-entry system uses:
  - financial documents, sales invoices
  - book of prime entry, sales day book
  - double-entry accounts in the general ledger
  - memorandum accounts in the sales ledger

■ Recording sales returns in the double-entry system uses:
  - financial documents, credit notes issued to customers
  - book of prime entry, sales returns day book
  - double-entry accounts in the general ledger
  - memorandum accounts in the sales ledger

financial documents	source documents for the accounting records
books of prime entry	the first accounting books in which transactions are recorded
coding	cross-referencing methods used to trace transactions through the accounting system
ledger	collection of accounts within the accounting system

debit entry	records a gain in value, an asset, or an expense
credit entry	records the giving of value, a liability, or an income item
sales	the sale of goods in which the business trades
revenue income	income from the goods in which the business trades
capital income	income from items other than the goods in which the business trades, eg a shop selling its old cash till
sales returns	goods previously sold on credit which are returned to the business by its customers
sales day book	book of prime entry prepared from sales invoices
sales returns day book	book of prime entry prepared from credit notes issued to customers
analysed sales day book	day books which incorporate analysis columns, for example between

- different departments
- different categories of goods sold, or services supplied

general ledger	ledger section which includes

- sales account
- sales returns account
- sales ledger control account
- Value Added Tax account

sales ledger	subsidiary ledger section which contains the memorandum accounts of the firm's receivables (customers)
memorandum account	a subsidiary ledger (eg sales ledger) account which provides a record of individual amounts (eg owing by receivables to the business)

Activities

3.1 Which one of the following is a book of prime entry?

(a)   sales day book

(b)   sales account

(c)   sales ledger account of T Smith

(d)   Value Added Tax account

Answer (a) or (b) or (c) or (d)

3.2 Which one of the following is in the right order?

(a)   sales invoice; sales day book; sales account; sales ledger control account; customer's account

(b)   sales day book; sales ledger control account; customer's account; sales account; sales invoice

(c)   sales day book; sales invoice; customer's account; sales account; sales ledger control account

(d)   sales account; sales ledger control account; customer's account; sales invoice; sales day book

Answer (a) or (b) or (c) or (d)

3.3 Explain in note format:

(a)   the principles of recording a credit sales transaction in the accounting system

(b)   the principles of recording a sales returns transaction in the accounting system

---

For Activities 3.4 and 3.5:

- work in pounds and pence, where appropriate

- the rate of Value Added Tax is to be calculated at 17.5% (when calculating VAT amounts, you should ignore fractions of a penny, ie round down to a whole penny)

- use a coding system incorporating the following:

sales day book	*– SDB50*	*general ledger account numbers*	
sales returns day book	*– SRDB18*	*sales ledger control account*	*– GL1200*
		sales account	*– GL4100*
sales ledger account numbers		*sales returns account*	*– GL4110*
A Cox	*– SL032*	*Value Added Tax account*	*– GL2200*
Dines Stores	*– SL048*		
E Grainger	*– SL055*		
M Kershaw	*– SL090*		
D Lloyd	*– SL095*		
Malvern Stores	*– SL110*		
Pershore Retailers	*– SL145*		
P Wilson	*– SL172*		

3.4   Wyvern Wholesalers sells office stationery to other businesses in the area. During April 20-5 the following credit transactions took place:

20-5

2 Apr	Sold goods to Malvern Stores £55 + VAT, invoice no 4578 issued
5 Apr	Sold goods to Pershore Retailers £65 + VAT, invoice no 4579 issued
7 Apr	Sold goods to E Grainger £28 + VAT, invoice no 4580 issued
9 Apr	Sold goods to P Wilson £58 + VAT, invoice no 4581 issued
12 Apr	Sold goods to M Kershaw £76 + VAT, invoice no 4582 issued
14 Apr	Sold goods to D Lloyd £66 + VAT, invoice no 4583 issued
19 Apr	Sold goods to A Cox £33 + VAT, invoice no 4584 issued
22 Apr	Sold goods to Dines Stores £102 + VAT, invoice no 4585 issued
23 Apr	Sold goods to Malvern Stores £47 + VAT, invoice no 4586 issued
26 Apr	Sold goods to P Wilson £35 + VAT, invoice no 4587 issued
29 Apr	Sold goods to A Cox £82 + VAT, invoice no 4588 issued

You are to:

(a)   Enter the above transactions in Wyvern Wholesaler's sales day book for April 20-5, using the format shown below.

(b)   Record the accounting entries in Wyvern Wholesaler's general ledger and sales ledger. (You will need to retain the ledger accounts for use with Activity 3.5.)

Sales Day Book						SDB50
Date	Details	Invoice number	Reference	Total £	VAT £	Net £

3.5 The following details are the sales returns of Wyvern Wholesalers for April 20-5. They are to be:

(a) entered in the sales returns day book for April 20-5, using the format shown below.

(b) recorded in the general ledger and sales ledger (use the ledgers already prepared in the answer to Activity 3.4)

20-5

8 Apr   Pershore Retailers returns goods £20 + VAT, credit note no 572 issued

12 Apr   E Grainger returns goods £28 + VAT, credit note no 573 issued

16 Apr   D Lloyd returns goods £33 + VAT, credit note no 574 issued

28 Apr   Malvern Stores returns goods £20 + VAT, credit note no 575 issued

30 Apr   A Cox returns goods £40 + VAT, credit note no 576 issued

Sales Returns Day Book						SDRB18
Date	Details	Credit note number	Reference	Total £	VAT £	Net £

3.6   You are employed by Johnson Limited as an accounts assistant. The business has a manual accounting system. Double-entry takes place in the general ledger; individual accounts of debtors are kept as memorandum accounts in the sales ledger. The VAT rate is 17.5%.

Notes:

- show your answer with a tick, words or figures, as appropriate
- coding is not required

(a)   The following transactions all took place on 30 June 20-9 and have been entered into the sales day book as shown below. No entries have yet been made into the ledger system.

Sales day book

Date 20-9	Details	Invoice number	Total £	VAT £	Net £
30 June	Bowne Ltd	610	940	140	800
30 June	Jamieson & Co	611	4,841	721	4,120
30 June	Pottertons	612	3,807	567	3,240
30 June	Wells plc	613	2,867	427	2,440
	Totals		12,455	1,855	10,600

What will be the entries in the general ledger?

General ledger

Account name	Amount £	Debit ✓	Credit ✓

What will be the entries in the sales ledger?

Sales ledger

Account name	Amount £	Debit ✓	Credit ✓

(b)   The following transactions all took place on 30 June 20-9 and have been entered into the sales returns day book as shown below. No entries have yet been made into the ledger system.

Sales returns day book

Date 20-9	Details	Credit note number	Total £	VAT £	Net £
30 June	Lloyd & Co	CN 47	564	84	480
30 June	Wyvern Stores	CN 48	1,222	182	1,040
	Totals		1,786	266	1,520

What will be the entries in the general ledger?

General ledger

Account name	Amount £	Debit ✓	Credit ✓

What will be the entries in the sales ledger?

Sales ledger

Account name	Amount £	Debit ✓	Credit ✓

3.7 The following is taken from the coding lists used at a business called Fashion Trading.

Customer	Sales ledger account code
Allens Stores	ALL001
Dart Enterprises	DAR001
Dennis & Co	DEN002
Eden Contracts	EDE001
Ginger Trading	GIN001
Jarvis & Co	JAR001
New Wave Fashions	NEW001
Number 1 Store	NUM002
Riverside Trading	RIV001
Toast Ltd	TOA001
Ye Olde Stores	YEO001

You are to set up the sales ledger account codes for the new customers shown below.

Customer	Sales ledger account code
Dymock Trading Co	
Hedgehog Fashions	
Jones & Co	

4 Process payments from customers

this chapter covers...

The earlier chapters of this book have explained how a business sets about selling its goods and services on credit, issuing invoices, credit notes and statements which help to ensure that the right money is received at the right time. The entry of these sales transactions into the book-keeping system has also been described.

This chapter will now explain the next stage in the process – the way in which a business will process a payment received from a customer who has bought goods on credit. It will continue the Case Study in Chapter 2 in which Cool Socks, a manufacturer of fashion socks, sold socks to Trends, a fashion store.

A payment sent by a business such as Trends in settlement of sales transactions will need to be checked and verified against documentation including:

- the remittance advice sent by the buyer and any payment sent by the buyer

- sales invoices and credit notes issued by the seller

- the statement of account sent by the seller

- the record of what is owing in the buyer's account in the sales ledger of the seller

In checking this documentation the seller will have to look out for any discrepancies which may be the result of an error made by the buyer, for example:

- an overpayment

- an underpayment

- the buyer taking settlement discount when the period for early payment has expired, or even when it is not offered

FINANCIAL DOCUMENTS – SOME REVISION

When a business makes a sale on credit terms it uses a number of financial documents which are sent to the buyer, these include:

- the **invoice**, which sets out the details of the sales transaction, including
  - the date
  - the sales price and any discount given
  - VAT (sales tax)
  - the total due
  - the date when payment is required (which is often 30 days after the date of the invoice)
- the **credit note**, which is used if any refund is due and can be deducted from the amount owing to the seller – for example a deduction made for faulty goods
- the **customer statement**, which sets out all the invoices and credit notes issued and any payments received over a set period (often a month), all resulting in a final amount due to be paid

FINANCIAL DOCUMENTS – REMITTANCE ADVICE

A further financial document which is important to the payment process is the **remittance advice**. This is an advice which can be posted, faxed or emailed, stating that a certain amount of money has been sent by a credit customer in settlement of an account. A remittance advice is used:

- **to accompany a cheque** – a practice which will decrease in use as the cheque is gradually phased out as a form of payment in the UK, or
- to advise the sending of a payment **direct to the seller's bank account** through **BACS**, the bank computer payment transfer system

These two types of remittance advice are illustrated on the next two pages. The remittance advices both relate to payments made to Cool Socks, the business introduced as a Case Study in Chapter 2. You will see that they both contain references. These are:

- the buyer's purchase order reference
- the seller's invoice number

Other details include the amount being sent and the means of payment, ie a cheque enclosed or payment direct to the bank account of the seller through the banks' computer network (known as a BACS payment). 'BACS' stands for 'Bankers Automated Clearing Services'.

remittance advice for a direct bank-to-bank BACS payment

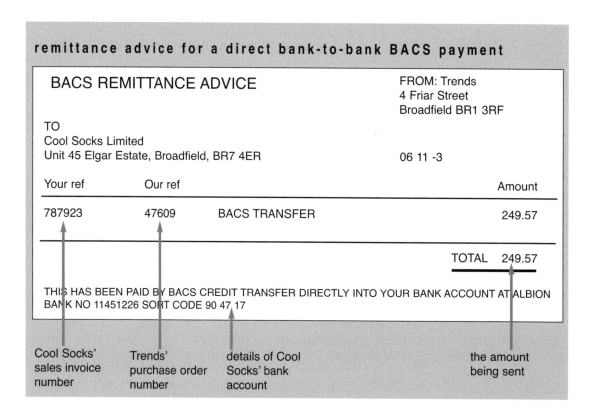

BACS remittance advice

- This remittance advice relates to a BACS bank transfer made by Trends in payment of their account with Cool Socks Limited. The advice has been posted, faxed or emailed from Trends' accounts department.

- The details do not include the invoice amount or the credit note amount, but only the final payment made. An alternative to this is to list the various documents (invoices, credit notes) which make up the payment. This method is shown on the remittance advice on the next page.

- The bank account details on the advice set out Cool Socks' bank account number and sort code in full. Some remittance advices may not provide the account number in full for security reasons

- Cool Socks will need to check its bank statement in due course to see if the payment has been received.

checks to be made

Cool Socks needs to check a number of details on this advice against the sales documentation and the sales ledger account of the customer making payment. This is to make sure that there are no errors or discrepancies and that the right amount has been sent for the right transactions. This process is explained in full in the Case Study on pages 74-77.

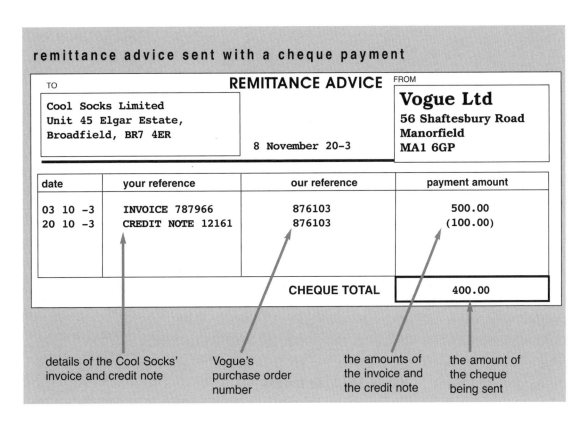

remittance advice sent with a cheque payment

		REMITTANCE ADVICE	
TO			FROM
Cool Socks Limited Unit 45 Elgar Estate, Broadfield, BR7 4ER		8 November 20-3	**Vogue Ltd** 56 Shaftesbury Road Manorfield MA1 6GP

date	your reference	our reference	payment amount
03 10 -3	INVOICE 787966	876103	500.00
20 10 -3	CREDIT NOTE 12161	876103	(100.00)
		CHEQUE TOTAL	400.00

details of the Cool Socks' invoice and credit note

Vogue's purchase order number

the amounts of the invoice and the credit note

the amount of the cheque being sent

remittance advice sent with a cheque

- This remittance advice is for a payment from Vogue Limited – a cheque for £400 – sent together through the post to Cool Socks.

- The advice shows the amounts of an invoice (£500) and a credit note (£100) taken account of when calculating the £400 payment.

- These details will help Cool Socks in their checking process which will involve the sales documentation and the sales ledger account for Vogue Limited.

- At the time of writing, cheques and BACS payments were both a common means of settling customer accounts. The use of cheques, however, will decline over time as they are gradually phased out as a means of payment.

- If a customer's cheque is received in payment, it will need to be checked carefully to make sure it is correctly written out.

checking the cheque

A **cheque** has to be in writing and signed by the customer paying the money. A cheque tells the customer's bank to pay a specified amount to a person or an organisation, know as the '**payee**.'

There are a number of important basic checks that a business needs to carry out when it receives a cheque as payment:

- is the cheque signed? – it is invalid if it is not
- is the payee's name correct? – it cannot be paid into the bank if it is not
- is the cheque in date? – a cheque becomes invalid after six months
- is the amount in words and figures the same?

The cheque below shows all these details:

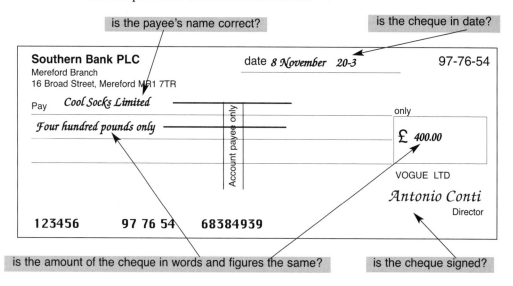

If the business (Cool Socks) accepting payment by cheque does not 'check' these important details before paying it in, the bank (Southern Bank) may refuse to pay it. If everything is in order, the amount of the cheque will be deducted from Cool Socks' bank account.

Now read the Case Study which follows. Note the internal checks that are made by Cool Socks when Trends settles its account.

Case Study

COOL SOCKS – PROCESSING THE PAYMENT

situation

Cool Socks Limited, a manufacturer of fashion socks, supplies Trends, a fashion store in Broadfield. In this Case Study, Trends sends a payment and remittance advice, which is checked by Cool Socks for errors and discrepancies.

The financial documents issued so far by Cool Socks are an invoice for socks supplied (see next page), a credit note for £27.73 (not illustrated) for some faulty socks returned and a statement of account sent to Trends at the end of the month (see page 76).

The amount due is £277.30 (invoice amount) minus £27.73 (credit note amount) = £249.57.

1.850

— INVOICE —

COOL SOCKS LIMITED

Unit 45 Elgar Estate, Broadfield, BR7 4ER
Tel 01908 765314 Fax 01908 765951 Email toni@cool.u-net.com
VAT Reg GB 0745 4672 76

invoice to

Trends **4 Friar Street** **Broadfield** **BR1 3RF**	

invoice no	787923
account	3993
your reference	47609
date/tax point	02 10 20-3

deliver to

as above

product code	description	quantity	price	unit	total	discount %	net
45B	Blue toebar socks	100	2.36	pair	236.00	0.00	236.00

terms
Net monthly
Carriage paid
E & OE

goods total	236.00
VAT	41.30
TOTAL	277.30

STATEMENT OF ACCOUNT

COOL SOCKS LIMITED

Unit 45 Elgar Estate, Broadfield, BR7 4ER
Tel 01908 765314 Fax 01908 765951 Email toni@cool.u-net.com
VAT REG GB 0745 4672 76

TO

Trends 4 Friar Street Broadfield BR1 3RF	account	3993
	date	31 10 20-3

date	details	debit £	credit £	balance £
01 10 20-3	Balance b/f	150.00		150.00
02 10 20-3	Payment received		150.00	00.00
02 10 20-3	Invoice 787923	277.30		277.30
10 10 20-3	Credit note 12157		27.73	249.57
	TOTAL			**249.57**

Notes on the statement and the ledger account

The statement of account illustrated above has four entries. The first two relate to full payment of last month's account (£150), and can be ignored. The last two relate to this Case Study and are highlighted by the grey boxes:

- the third entry is the invoice for £277.30 issued on 2 October to Trends
- the last entry is the credit note for £27.73 issued on 10 October to Trends

The amount owed by Trends to Cool Socks (the account balance) is £249.57

These entries have also been entered by Cool Socks in the double-entry accounting system, in the **sales ledger account** for Trends shown below.

Debit	Sales Ledger: Trends Account						Credit	
20-3	Details	£	p	20-3	Details	£	p	
1 Oct	Balance b/d	150	00	2 Oct	Bank	150	00	
2 Oct	Sales	277	30	10 Oct	Sales returns	27	73	

receipt of the remittance advice

On 6 November Cool Socks received a remittance advice (shown below) from Trends stating that £249.57 has been paid into the bank account of Cool Socks Limited by BACS transfer – ie a direct computer payment rather than a cheque.

What checks should Cool Socks make to make sure the payment of £249.57 is correct and valid?

BACS REMITTANCE ADVICE

FROM: Trends
4 Friar Street
Broadfield BR1 3RF

TO
Cool Socks Limited
Unit 45 Elgar Estate, Broadfield, BR7 4ER

06 11 20-3

Your ref	Our ref		Amount
787923	47609	BACS TRANSFER	249.57

TOTAL 249.57

THIS HAS BEEN PAID BY BACS CREDIT TRANSFER DIRECTLY INTO YOUR BANK ACCOUNT AT ALBION BANK NO 11451226 SORT CODE 90 47 17

solution

The following checks could be made by the accounts staff of Cool Socks.

Question   Are the remittance advice references correct?

Answer   Check the original documentation. The answer is 'Yes'.

- Invoice number 787923 (see page 75) agrees with the 'Your ref 787923' of the remittance advice.

- The Trends purchase order number 47609 (to be found in the Cool Socks filing system) is quoted on the remittance advice.

Question   Is the remittance advice amount of £249.57 correct? Answer is 'Yes'.

Answer   Invoice value £277.30 minus credit note value £27.73 = £249.57

This can be verified from the statement issued by Cool Socks on 31 October and also from the sales ledger account of Trends in the books of Cool Socks. Both (see opposite page) show the two figures (£277.30 and £27.73) which result in the total owing figure of £249.57.

Note that Cool Socks would not need to carry out <u>all</u> these checks, but a minimum requirement is likely to be:

- a check of the documentation references (especially the invoice number), <u>and</u>
- a calculation of the amount paid – from figures obtained from the customer statement issued <u>or</u> from the sales ledger account

DEALING WITH DISCREPANCIES

The Case Study on the previous four pages has explained the checks that should be made by the seller when a remittance advice is received from a credit customer. In this example, all was correct. Normally this is the case, but there are situations where references do not tie up or, more often, the amount is wrong. These **discrepancies** can occur when:

- there is an **underpayment** – not enough money has been received
- there is an **overpayment** – too much money has been received
- the buyer has made a mistake when deducting **settlement discount**

We will deal with each of these in turn.

underpayments

There are number of reasons why a credit customer may not send enough money when settling an account. These are described below, together with the action that should be taken in each case by the seller.

reason	the customer has made a genuine mistake with the figures
solution	the seller should contact the customer (by telephone or email), and politely explain the problem; the customer should be asked for an adjusting payment or advised that it will be adjusted for in the next statement
reason	the customer has not paid all the due invoices because there is a dispute over one of them
solution	the seller should contact the customer and attempt to resolve the problem; if necessary the matter may have to be referred to a line manager

overpayments

There are number of reasons why a credit customer may send too much money when settling an account. This is not a common experience! These reasons are described below and appropriate solutions are suggested.

reason	the customer has made a genuine mistake with the figures
solution	the seller should contact the customer and explain the situation; the ideal solution for the seller is to keep the extra money and wait for the next statement to make the necessary adjustment; it is possible that the customer may want the money (it may be a large amount), in which case an adjusting payment may need to be made

reason   the customer has ignored a credit note or has paid an invoice twice in error

solution   the seller should contact the customer and explain the situation; the ideal solution for the seller is to retain the extra money and wait for the next statement to make the necessary adjustment, unless the customer urgently needs the money, in which case an adjusting payment will need to be made promptly

discrepancies with settlement discount

Settlement discount is an 'early payment discount' where a seller allows a customer to deduct a percentage discount from the invoice total if payment is made within a specified period of time, eg seven days.

Settlement discount is explained on pages 28-29. If you are unsure about this rather complicated procedure you should read these pages again. The main problem with settlement discount is that it is not normally calculated and taken into account on the invoice itself, but the calculation is left to the customer. This is where errors can occur. When a business offers settlement discount, it is set out in the 'Terms' section at the bottom of the invoice, eg:

Settlement discount of 2.5% for payment within 7 days of the invoice date.

If the goods total before VAT is £100, the discount available if the invoice is paid within 7 days of the invoice is (£100 x 2.5)/100 = £2.50.

The correct total amount actually payable is therefore:

$$£100 \text{ minus } £2.50 \qquad = \quad £97.50$$
$$\text{plus VAT @ 17.5\% on £97.50} \qquad = \quad £17.06$$
$$= \quad \underline{£114.56}$$

To confuse the issue, the final total of the invoice sent to the customer is:

$$\text{goods total } \underline{\text{before discount is taken}} \ = £100.00$$
$$\text{plus VAT on £97.50 (not on £100)} \ = \quad £17.06$$
$$= \quad \underline{£117.06}$$

As you can see from this, there is plenty of room for customer error:

• the amount of discount calculated by the customer may be incorrect

• the customer may take the discount after the seven days has elapsed

• the customer may take a discount when it is not being offered at all

In each of these three cases, the seller will have to contact the customer and explain the nature of the discrepancy. Examples of these errors are shown in the Case Study which follows on the next page.

<table>
<tr><td>Case
Study</td></tr>
</table>

1,850

1,600

SETTLEMENT DISCOUNT DISCREPANCIES

situation

You work in the accounts department of Cool Socks Limited. The company offers to some (but not all) customers a settlement discount of 2.5% on invoices which are paid within 7 days of the invoice date.

When settlement discount is made available, the 'Terms' section at the bottom of the invoice always states:

"Settlement discount of 2.5% for payment within 7 days of the invoice date."

The date is 25 November and you have to check three invoices which have had settlement discount deducted by the customer. Your line manager asks you to report and correct any discrepancies you can find. The current VAT rate is 17.5%.

Invoice 1 – payment amount received £1,120.62

Dated 22 November. Terms indicate that 2.5% settlement discount is available for payment within 7 days. Goods total is £1,000 and discount deducted is £50. VAT on the invoice is £170.62.

Invoice 2 – payment amount received £458.25

Dated 8 November. Terms indicate that 2.5% settlement discount is available for payment within 7 days. Goods total is £400 and the discount deducted is £10. VAT is £68.25.

Invoice 3 – payment amount received £287.50

Dated 22 November. There is no mention of a 2.5% settlement discount in the 'Terms' section of the invoice. Goods total is £250 and VAT is £43.75. Cash discount of £6.25 has been taken by the customer.

---

solution

Answers

Invoice 1: the discount deducted is calculated at 5% (£50) and should be at 2.5% (£25). The payment should be £975 + VAT £170.62 = £1,145.62.

Invoice 2: the 7 day period for deduction of settlement discount has expired and therefore no discount should be deducted. The payment should have been £400 + VAT of £68.25 = £468.25. Note that the VAT is calculated on the £390 and not on the £400, whether or not the discount is taken.

Invoice 3: there is no settlement discount available on this invoice but, despite this, the customer has taken 2.5% (£6.25). The payment should have been £293.75.

Chapter Summary

- When a customer who has bought goods or services on credit makes payment of the account, the customer will send a **remittance advice** to the seller.

- Payment may be received by cheque or through the BACS, the bank computer-based payment transfer system.

- When a remittance advice is received it must be checked carefully against the sales documentation held by the seller and the customer's account in the seller's sales ledger. The amount received must be the correct amount. The documentation checked includes invoices, credit notes and the remittance advice itself.

- If a cheque is received it must be checked to ensure that it is valid.

- If payment is made through the BACS, the bank statement must be checked in due course to confirm that the payment has been received.

- Discrepancies relating to payments received can be caused by:
  - **underpayments** – a disputed invoice may not have been included
  - **overpayments** – a credit note may have been ignored or an invoice paid twice
  - problems with **settlement discount** – discount rate incorrect, discount period expired, no discount available

- In all cases the discrepancies must be communicated to the customer so that an appropriate adjustment can be made.

Key Terms

remittance advice	an advice received from a customer telling the seller that a payment has been made
BACS	Bankers Automated Clearing Services – a bank computer-based system which makes payment direct from one bank account to another
settlement discount	a percentage reduction in the selling price given to the buyer if the buyer pays within a specified short space of time; this discount is also known as 'cash' discount

Activities

4.1   A business which receives a remittance advice from a customer is likely to check it against the following documents or accounts:

(a)   delivery note, invoice, customer statement

(b)   delivery note, invoice, sales ledger account

(c)   invoice, purchase order, customer statement

(d)   invoice, sales ledger account, customer statement

Which of the above options is correct?

4.2   On an invoice which offers settlement discount:

(a)   the settlement discount calculation is always shown

(b)   the settlement discount percentage is shown

(c)   the VAT (sales tax) is worked out on the goods total before the settlement discount is deducted

(d)   the final invoice total takes into account the settlement discount deducted

Which of the above options is correct?

4.3   On the next three pages are set out remittance advices and associated documents.

You are to check the remittance advices against the documents and

1   identify and describe any discrepancies that you find

2   suggest the action that could be taken by the supplier in each case

4.3 (a)

remittance advice sent to the seller

BACS REMITTANCE ADVICE	FROM: Trends
	4 Friar Street
	Broadfield BR1 3RF

TO
Cool Socks Limited
Unit 45 Elgar Estate, Broadfield, BR7 4ER   06 12 20-3

Your ref	Our ref		Amount
788101	47645	BACS TRANSFER	490.00

TOTAL   490.00

THIS HAS BEEN PAID BY BACS CREDIT TRANSFER DIRECTLY INTO YOUR BANK ACCOUNT AT ALBION
BANK NO 11451226 SORT CODE 90 47 17

statement sent by the seller to the customer

STATEMENT OF ACCOUNT
COOL SOCKS LIMITED
Unit 45 Elgar Estate, Broadfield, BR7 4ER
Tel 01908 765314 Fax 01908 765951 Email toni@cool.u-net.com
VAT REG GB 0745 4672 76

TO

Trends
4 Friar Street
Broadfield
BR1 3RF

account   **3993**

date   **30 11 20-3**

date	details	debit £	credit £	balance £
01 11 20-3	Balance b/f	249.57		249.57
02 11 20-3	Payment received		249.57	00.00
02 10 20-3	Invoice 788101	490.00		490.00
10 10 20-3	Credit note 12189		49.00	441.00
			TOTAL	**441.00**

4.3 (b)

remittance advice sent to the seller

TO	REMITTANCE ADVICE	FROM
Cool Socks Limited Unit 45 Elgar Estate, Broadfield, BR7 4ER	8 November 20–3	**Vogue Ltd** **56 Shaftesbury Road** **Manorfield** **MA1 6GP**

date	your reference	our reference	payment amount
03 11 –3	INVOICE 788106	876213	500.00
15 11 –3	INVOICE 788256	876287	220.10
20 11 –3	CREDIT NOTE 12218	876287	(22.01)
		TOTAL	**698.09**

sales ledger account of the customer in the accounting records of the seller

Debit				Vogue Limited		Credit	
20-3	**Details**	**£**	**p**	**20-3**	**Details**	**£**	**p**
3 Nov	Sales	500	00	10 Oct	Sales returns	22	01
15 Nov	Sales	220	10				
17 Nov	Sales	625	85				

4.3 (c)

remittance advice sent to the seller

BACS REMITTANCE ADVICE

FROM:
RTC Fashions
85 Fish Street
Stourminster ST1 8RT

TO
Chico Importers
34 Oldfield Street, London EC1 6TR

03 12 20-3

Your ref	Our ref		Amount
10956	1078	BACS TRANSFER Invoice 10956 less 5% settlement discount	625.10
			TOTAL 625.10

THIS HAS BEEN PAID BY BACS CREDIT TRANSFER DIRECTLY INTO YOUR BANK ACCOUNT AT HRBC BANK ACCOUNT NO xxxx6534 SORT CODE 40 47 17

invoice sent to the seller

INVOICE

CHICO IMPORTERS

34 Oldfield Street, London EC1 6TR
Tel 0208765322 Fax 0208765564 Email sales@chicoimporters.com
VAT Reg GB 0745 4672 76

invoice to

RTC Fashions
85 Fish Street
Stourminster
ST1 8RT

invoice no	10956
account	834
your reference	1078
date/tax point	5 11 20-3

product code	description	quantity	price	unit	total	discount %	net
5674R	T shirts (red)	200	3.50	each	700.00	20.00	560.00

goods total	560.00

terms
Net monthly
Carriage paid

VAT	98.00
TOTAL	658.00

5 Process documents from suppliers

In Chapter 2 we described the financial documents prepared by a **seller** of goods and services on credit. This chapter looks at the situation from the purchaser's point of view and describes the procedures and documents involved when goods and services are **bought** on credit.

The chapter covers the following areas:

*   the use of financial documents for the purchase of goods and services – purchase invoice, delivery note, goods received note, credit note

*   the checking of the supplier's documents received against the purchaser's documents

*   the calculation of document totals, including discounts and VAT (sales tax)

*   the coding and filing of documents

*   the checking and authorisation of documents

*   dealing with discrepancies

This chapter covers the treatment of documents until payment is made. The processes of calculating and making payment are covered in Chapter 7.

BUSINESS DOCUMENTS – THE PURCHASER'S POINT OF VIEW

When a business **sells** goods and services its main concern is that it provides what has been ordered and that it gets paid on time. When a business **orders** goods and services, on the other hand, it will want to ensure that:

- the correct goods and services are provided – on time
- they are charged at the right price

The traditional procedure is for the purchaser to accumulate on file – often stapled together – a series of documents which will be checked against each other as they are produced or come into the office, eg copy purchase order, delivery note, goods received note, invoice, credit note, statement, and so on. These will often be kept in a 'pending invoices' file until payment is made, when they will go into a 'paid invoices' file - as shown in the diagram below.

This chapter covers the treatment of documents until payment is made. Calculating and making payment is covered in Chapter 7.

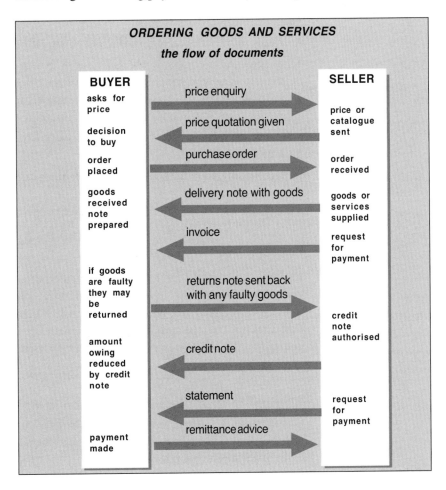

ORDERING PROCEDURES

the traditional method

The diagram on the previous page shows the traditional method of ordering goods and services: a purchase order is issued, the goods (or services) are delivered (or provided) and an invoice is sent which is eventually paid by the customer. There are of course, many variations on this procedure, with the introduction of e-commerce where buying and selling and payment takes place on-line.

In this book and in your studies the emphasis is on the traditional method of ordering and paying because the principles of this method underlie all the other methods. You should however be aware of the other methods as you are likely to encounter them in your day-to-day work.

other ordering methods – paper based

Businesses can order goods and services in a variety of other ways:

- filling in a catalogue order form and posting it to the seller with payment
- telephoning a company which is selling to you for the first time to ask them to issue you with a 'pro-forma invoice' for the goods or service you need; when you receive this invoice document, you will send it back with payment and the goods or service will be supplied by return
- faxing off a catalogue order form and quoting the company debit card or credit card details
- telephoning an order and quoting the company debit or credit card details

other ordering methods – electronically based

Electronic ordering has been made possible through EDI (Electronic Data Interchange) and e-commerce.

EDI (Electronic Data Interchange) is a method of connecting businesses by computer link so that documents such as purchase orders and invoices can be electronically generated and payments made electronically when they are due. EDI has been running for many years, the electronic links are private and secure; the system is expensive to set up. Supermarkets, for example, commonly use EDI.

e-commerce

E-commerce is a loose term which is short for 'electronic commerce'. It covers selling and buying on the internet, both business-to business and also by individual personal customers.

documents for purchases

This chapter concentrates on the traditional method of purchasing based on paper documents. This is not to say that electronic methods are any different; they are very much based on the same principles. The documents we will describe are:

- purchase order
- delivery note
- goods received note
- purchase invoice

When a business purchases goods, it is important that the accounting system includes checks and controls to ensure that:

- the correct goods have been received in an acceptable condition
- the correct terms (including discounts) and price have been applied
- the goods are paid for once only (paying for goods twice does occur!)

PURCHASE ORDER

A purchaser, when the price of the product has been agreed, normally issues a **purchase order**. It is essential that this purchase order is **authorised** by the appropriate person. This authority is shown on the document in the form of a signature and date. Some businesses will insist that more senior staff in the buying department sign larger orders. A business keeps a copy of every purchase order it issues and often files them in numerical order (each order has a numerical code). The purchase order for Blue Toebar socks from the Cool Socks Case Study in Chapter 2 is shown below.

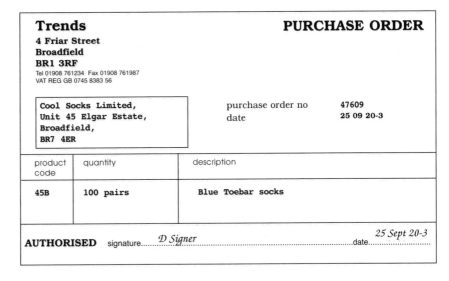

Trends		PURCHASE ORDER	
4 Friar Street Broadfield BR1 3RF Tel 01908 761234 Fax 01908 761987 VAT REG GB 0745 8383 56			
Cool Socks Limited, Unit 45 Elgar Estate, Broadfield, BR7 4ER		purchase order no date	47609 25 09 20-3
product code	quantity	description	
45B	100 pairs	Blue Toebar socks	
AUTHORISED signature...... *D Signer*			date...... *25 Sept 20-3* ......

DELIVERY NOTE

When the goods ordered are despatched by the seller they will normally be accompanied by a **delivery note**.

The delivery note shown below was described in the Cool Socks Case Study in Chapter 2. The main features are as follows:

- The delivery note has a numerical reference (here it is 68873), useful for filing and later reference if there is a query.

- The method of delivery is stated – here the delivery is by parcel carrier.

- The delivery note quotes the purchase order number – 47609 – this enables the buyer to 'tie up' the delivery with the original purchase order.

- The delivery note quotes:
  - Cool Socks' catalogue reference 45B as the product code
  - the quantity supplied
  - the description of the goods, but no price – it is not needed at this stage

  These details will be checked against the goods themselves straightaway so that any discrepancies can be reported without delay.

  If the business purchasing the goods uses a **goods received note** (see next page) this will be completed at this stage.

- The delivery note will be signed and dated by the person receiving the goods as proof of delivery. This signature process can also be carried out electronically – the person receiving the goods will be asked to sign a portable electronic device.

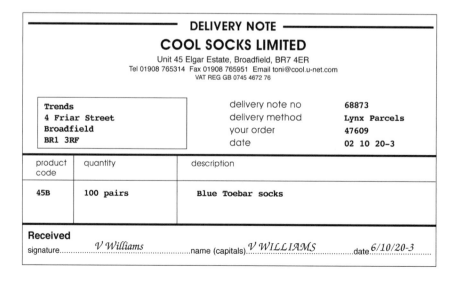

GOODS RECEIVED NOTE

Some businesses use an internal document known as a **goods received note** (**GRN**). The buyer records on this document the receipt of the goods and the details set out on the delivery note or advice note sent by the supplier.

The GRN is essentially a checklist on which is recorded:

- the name of the supplier
- the quantity and details of the goods ordered
- the purchase order number
- the name of the carrier and any carrier reference number

As the goods are received and checked in, the GRN is ticked and signed to indicate that the right quantity and description of goods has been received.

The GRN forms part of the payment authorisation process: only when a completed and correct GRN is approved by the Accounts Department can the relevant invoice be paid.

Shown below is the goods received note relating to the Case Study in Chapter 2 in which the shop 'Trends' ordered some fashion socks from Cool Socks Limited.

Note that the receipt of the 100 pairs of socks has been recorded, and also the fact that 10 pairs are damaged.

Trends		**GOODS RECEIVED NOTE**	
Supplier			
Cool Socks Limited, Unit 45 Elgar Estate, Broadfield, BR7 4ER	GRN no date	1871 05 10 20-3	
quantity	description		order number
100 pairs	Blue Toebar socks		47609
carrier Lynx Parcels		consignment no 8479347	
received by *V Williams*		checked by *R Patel*	
condition of goods (please tick and comment)	good condition damaged ✔ (10 pairs) shortages		**copies to** Buyer ✔ Accounts ✔ Stockroom ✔

PURCHASE INVOICE

You will already be very familiar with the **purchase invoice** because it is the **sales invoice** sent out by the person selling the goods or services. In the Chapter 2 Case Study the sales invoice sent out by Cool Socks becomes the purchase invoice received by Trends, the buyer:

━━ INVOICE ━━

COOL SOCKS LIMITED
Unit 45 Elgar Estate, Broadfield, BR7 4ER
Tel 01908 765314 Fax 01908 765951 Email toni@cool.u-net.com
VAT Reg GB 0745 4672 76

invoice to

Trends
4 Friar Street
Broadfield
BR1 3RF

invoice no	787923
account	3993
your reference	47609
date/tax point	02 10 20-3

deliver to

as above

product code	description	quantity	price	unit	total	discount %	net
45B	Blue toebar socks	100	2.36	pair	236.00	0.00	236.00

terms
Net monthly
Carriage paid
E & OE

goods total	236.00
VAT	41.30
TOTAL	277.30

CHECKING INVOICE, DELIVERY NOTE AND PURCHASE ORDER

Now that you are familiar with all the purchase documents we will explain the checking process that will need to be made by the purchaser. This involves two separate procedures carried out in the Accounts Department:

- checking the documents – the invoice, delivery note (or GRN) and copy purchase order – with each other
- checking the calculations on the invoice

We will deal with these in separate stages, starting with the checking of the documents:

check 1 – goods received and delivery note

When the goods are received they should be checked against the delivery note – the quantities should be counted and the condition of the goods checked and noted on a GRN if required. Any discrepancies or damage should be notified immediately to the supplier so that replacements can be sent or the buyer credited with the value of the missing or damaged goods (ie the bill reduced by the issue of a credit note).

check 2 – delivery note and purchase order

The delivery note should then be checked in the Accounts Department against a copy of the original purchase order (see illustration on page 95):

- supplier catalogue number – has the right type of goods been delivered?
- quantity – has the right number been delivered?
- specifications – are the goods delivered to the same specifications as those ordered?
- purchase order reference number – do the goods relate to the purchase order being examined?

If all is in order, the delivery note will be filed with the copy purchase order under the purchase order reference number, ready for checking against the invoice when it arrives.

check 3 – invoice, delivery note and purchase order

When the invoice eventually arrives from the supplier, it should be checked against the delivery note and the purchase order (which should be filed together). The specific points to look at are:

- **invoice and delivery note**
  Are the details of the goods on the invoice and delivery note the same? The product code, description and quantity of the goods should agree.

- **invoice and purchase order**

  Has the correct price been charged? The unit price quoted by the supplier or obtained from the supplier's catalogue will be stated on the purchase order, and should agree with the unit price stated on the invoice. If there is a difference, it should be queried with the supplier.

student task

Look at the invoice below and the purchase order and delivery note on the next page. They all relate to the same transaction. Can you spot any discrepancies? The answers are set out at the bottom of this page.

━━━ **INVOICE** ━━━

Stourford Office Supplies

Unit 12, Avon Industrial Estate, Stourford, SF5 6TD
Tel 01807 765434 Fax 01807 765123 Email stourford@stourford.co.uk
VAT Reg GB 0745 4001 76

invoice to

Martley Machine Rental Limited 67 Broadgreen Road Martley MR6 7TR	

invoice no	652771
account	MAR435
your reference	47780

deliver to

as above

date/tax point	31 03 20-3

product code	description	quantity	price	unit	total	discount %	net
3564748	80gsm white Supalaser	15	3.50	ream	52.00	0.00	52.00

terms
Net monthly
Carriage paid
E & OE

goods total	52.00
VAT	9.01
TOTAL	42.99

The purchase order and delivery note agree, but the invoice has a number of discrepancies:
- the order reference differs (47700 and 47780)
- the product code differs (3564749 and 3564748)
- the product description differs (100 gsm and 80 gsm)
- the price differs (£4.00 and £3.50 per ream)

Martley Machine Rental

PURCHASE ORDER

67 Broadgreen Road
Martley
MR6 7TR
Tel 01908 546321 Fax 01908 546335
VAT REG GB 0745 8383 56

Stourford Office Supplies	purchase order no	47700
Unit 12	date	13 03 20-3
Avon Industrial Estate		
Stourford SF5 6TD		

product code	quantity	description	
3564749	15 reams	100gsm white Supalaser paper @ £4.00 per ream	

AUTHORISED   signature............ *C Farmer* ....date............ *13 March 20-3* ....

catalogue number | quantity | order specifications | purchase order reference number

---

— DELIVERY NOTE —

Stourford Office Supplies

Unit 12, Avon Industrial Estate, Stourford, SF5 6TD
Tel 01807 765434 Fax 01807 765123 Email stourford@stourford.co.uk
VAT Reg GB 0745 4001 76

Martley Machine Rental Ltd	delivery note no	26754
67 Broadgreen Road	delivery method	Puma Express
Martley	your order	47700
MR6 7TR	date	27 03 20-3

product code	quantity	description
3564749	15 reams	100gsm white Supalaser paper

Received
signature................ *G.Hughes* ....print name (capitals)...*G.HUGHES*................date.*31.03.20-3*

details to check on the purchase order and delivery note

CHECKING THE CALCULATIONS ON THE INVOICE

Another important step is for the Accounts Department to check the calculations on the invoice. If any one of these calculations is incorrect, the final total will be wrong, and the invoice will have to be queried with the supplier, so accurate checking is essential. The checks to be made are:

quantity x unit price The quantity of the items multiplied by the unit price must be correct. The result – the total price or 'price extension' – is used for the calculation of any trade discount applicable.

trade or bulk discount Any trade or bulk discount – allowances given to approved trade customers or for bulk purchases – must be deducted from the total price worked out. Trade or bulk discount is calculated as a percentage of the total price, eg a trade discount of 20% on a total price of £150 is calculated:

£150 x $\frac{20}{100}$ = £30

The net price charged (before VAT) is therefore

£150 – £30 = £120 = net total

settlement discount Any settlement (cash) discount – an allowance sometimes given for quick payment – is deducted from the net total before VAT is calculated. Settlement discount, when it is offered, is usually included as one of the terms at the bottom of the invoice. It is not deducted from the invoice total, so it will be up to the buyer to settle early and to adjust the invoice total down.

VAT Value Added Tax (a sales tax) in this book is calculated at 17.5%. To calculate VAT, the total after the deduction of any settlement discount is treated as follows

Total x $\frac{17.5}{100}$ = VAT amount

If you are using a calculator, all you need to do is to multiply the total by 0.175 to give the VAT, which is then added to the total.

Note that fractions of a penny are ignored. If the total price is £55.75, the VAT will be:

$$£55.75 \times 0.175 = £9.75625$$

£9.75625 then loses the last three digits – the fraction of a penny – to become £9.75.

For the purpose of your studies you must assume that the calculations on all invoices must be checked. In practice, computerised invoicing performs the calculations automatically, and in principle should be correct.

Now check the calculations on the invoice on page 94. You should be able to detect a large number of errors:

- quantity x unit price should be £52.50, not £52.00

- the VAT is wrongly calculated £52.00 x 0.175 = £9.10, not £9.01 (it would be £9.18 on £52.50)

- the VAT has been deducted instead of added: the total should be £52.50 + £9.18 = £61.68

RETURNS – CHECKING CREDIT NOTES

A purchaser will sometimes have to return faulty or incorrect goods and request a credit note from the seller to reduce the amount owed.

Note that a purchaser should never for this reason change figures on an invoice – this would cause havoc with the accounting records! When goods are sent back they are normally returned with a **returns note** which sets out all the details of the goods.

Trends			**RETURNS NOTE**
4 Friar Street			
Broadfield			
BR1 3RF			
Tel 01908 761234 Fax 01908 761987			
VAT REG GB 0745 8383 56			

Cool Socks Limited,	returns note no	2384
Unit 45 Elgar Estate,	date	**08 10 20-3**
Broadfield,		
BR7 4ER		

product code	quantity	description
45B	10 pairs	Blue Toebar socks

REASON FOR RETURN: *faulty goods, credit requested*

SIGNATURE　*R SINGH*　　　　　DATE　*10 10 20-3*

When the goods are received back by the seller and checked, a **credit note** will be issued to reduce the amount owing. The credit note from the Cool Socks Case Study is illustrated below.

CHECKING THE CREDIT NOTE

When the **credit note** is received by the purchaser it will have to be checked carefully to make sure that the quantity of goods, the price, discount and VAT are correctly calculated. It will be checked against the **goods received note** if one has been issued (not all businesses do), or the returns note or other internal records to make sure that the discrepancy has been properly resolved – ie has full credit been given for damaged/missing/incorrect goods?

If the credit note is correct, the document will be entered into the accounting records and then filed with (stapled to) the appropriate copy purchase order, delivery note, invoice, GRN or copy returns note, awaiting the arrival of the statement.

——————— CREDIT NOTE ———————

COOL SOCKS LIMITED

Unit 45 Elgar Estate, Broadfield, BR7 4ER
Tel 01908 765314 Fax 01908 765951 Email toni@cool.u-net.com
VAT REG GB 0745 4672 76

to

Trends 4 Friar Street Broadfield BR1 3RF	

credit note no	12157
account	3993
your reference	47609
our invoice	787923
date/tax point	13 10 20-3

product code	description	quantity	price	unit	total	discount %	net
45B	Blue Toebar socks	10	2.36	pair	23.60	0.00	23.60

Reason for credit
10 pairs of socks received damaged
(Your returns note no. R/N 2384)

GOODS TOTAL	23.60
VAT	4.13
TOTAL	27.73

Trends		**GOODS RECEIVED NOTE**	

Supplier

Cool Socks Limited, Unit 45 Elgar Estate, Broadfield, BR7 4ER	GRN no date	**1871** **05 10 20-3**

quantity	description	order number
100 pairs	**Blue Toebar socks**	47609

carrier	**Lynx Parcels**	consignment no 8479347

received by	*V Williams*	checked by	*R Patel*

condition of goods (please tick and comment)	good condition damaged ✔ (10 pairs) shortages	**copies to** Buyer ✔ Accounts ✔ Stockroom ✔

goods received note – details to check

If you compare the **credit note** on the opposite page and the **goods received note** shown above you will see that the following details can be checked:

- the identity of the goods returned – here it is blue Toebar socks
- the quantity returned – ten pairs of socks in this case
- the purchase order reference number – here it is 47609

As you will see, all is correct and so it is in order for Trends to make payment for this transaction on the due date.

The processes for preparing for payment of purchasers' accounts will be dealt with in full in Chapter 7.

CODING PURCHASES INVOICES AND CREDIT NOTES

the need to code

When a business processes invoices and credit notes received from suppliers it will usually code them so that they can be entered into the accounting system quickly and easily. This will be very useful, for example, if a computer accounting system is used. Normally two different sets of codes will be used

- a **supplier account** code which will identify the supplier of the goods or services – this code may be alphabetic, alpha-numeric or numeric; if letters are involved they usually relate to the first few letters of the name of the supplier

- a **general ledger account** code which will identify the account which will be debited in the accounting system – it normally relates to the type of purchases made or expenses paid; it may be alpha-numeric or numeric

You will see from the purchases invoice and credit note on the opposite page that the codes may be entered in boxes imprinted onto the document by a rubber stamp used by the buyer (see the grey arrows indicating the boxes).

using the account code lists

The business will keep account lists to hand so that accounts staff can quickly look up the appropriate code. As noted above, these will be for

- supplier accounts

- general ledger accounts

Extracts from these two types of account lists are shown below, Note that the account names are sorted in alphabetical order:

Supplier	Supplier code
Jarma Supplies	JA006
John Taylor Limited	JO004
Labtech Limited	LA001
Liverpool Kitware	LI001

Item	General Ledger code
Shades	5045
T-shirts	5060
Trainers	5100
Trousers	5210

The **invoice** on the next page has therefore been given the following codes:

Supplier code JA006 for Jarma Supplies

General ledger code 5060 for T-shirts

The **credit note** on the next page has been given the following codes:

Supplier code LA001 for Labtech Limited

General ledger code 5045 for Shades

INVOICE

JARMA SUPPLIES

Advent House, Otto Way
New Milton, SR1 6TF
Tel 01722 295875 Fax 01722 295611 Email sales@johnsonthreads.co.uk
VAT Reg GB 01982 6865 06

invoice to

RT Fashionware
34, Tennyson High Road
Maidstone
ME4 5EW

invoice no	7736
account	94122
your reference	675
date/tax point	01 04 20-7

description	quantity	price	unit	total
Max T-shirts (red)	200	3.00	each	600.00

terms
30 days
Carriage paid
E & OE

Supplier a/c reference	general ledger a/c number
JA006	5060

goods total	600.00
VAT	105.00
TOTAL	705.00

coding details

CREDIT NOTE

LABTECH LIMITED

Unit 7 Roughway Estate,
Martley Road, Cookford, CO1 9GH
Tel 01843 265432 Fax 01843 265439 Email accounts@fabtech.co.uk
VAT Reg GB 0877 9333 06

to

RT Fashionware
34, Tennyson High Road
Maidstone
ME4 5EW

credit note no	976
account	94122
your reference	47601
date/tax point	12 04 20-7

description	quantity	price	unit	total
Monaco shades 2744	5	30.00	each	150.00

reason for credit:
lenses damaged

supplier a/c reference	general ledger a/c number
LA001	5045

goods total	150.00
VAT	26.25
TOTAL	176.25

Chapter Summary

■ When a business orders goods or services on credit, it may do so using a manual paper-based system or by using an electronic system (either EDI or e-commerce).

■ When a business orders goods on credit using a manual paper-based system it will deal with a number of financial documents:
- the purchase order
- the delivery note
- the goods received note
- the purchase invoice

■ It is important that a series of checks are made to the financial documents to ensure that the goods or services provided are the correct ones, charged at the right price. The checks will involve calculations and references.

■ If a discrepancy is found, it should be noted and the seller contacted so that the account of the purchaser can be credited and the amount owing reduced accordingly.

■ Purchases invoices and credit notes should be coded with the supplier account and general ledger account codes so that they can easily be entered into the accounting system.

Key Terms

EDI	Electronic Data Interchange (EDI) is an electronic system of ordering goods and services using secure private computer links
e-commerce	buying and selling on the Internet by businesses and personal customers
purchase order	a document issued and authorised by the buyer of goods and services, sent to the seller, indicating the goods or services required
delivery note	a document listing and accompanying the goods sent to the purchaser
goods received note	a document used by purchasers to record receipt of inventory (stock) and any returns made
purchases invoice	a document issued by the seller of goods or services to the purchaser indicating the amount owing and the required payment date
returns note	a document sent to the supplier with any faulty goods
credit note	a document issued by the seller of goods or services to the purchaser reducing the amount owing

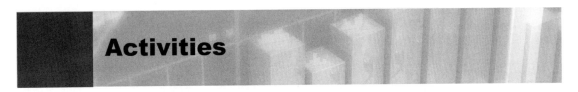

Activities

5.1   What type of business document would normally be used when goods are bought on credit

(a)   to order the goods from the seller?

(b)   to accompany goods sent from the seller?

(c)   to record the receipt and any discrepancies relating to the goods at the buyer's premises?

(d)   to advise the buyer in the first instance of the amount of money due?

(e)   to advise the buyer that a reduction is being made in the buyer's account for faulty goods supplied?

5.2   What is the difference between a delivery note and a goods received note?

5.3   Which documents would normally be checked by the buyer against the purchase order? Answer (a) or (b) or (c) or (d).

(a)   the delivery note and the invoice

(b)   the invoice and the returns note

(c)   the goods received note and the returns note

(d)   the returns note and the delivery note

5.4   What document would a buyer expect to receive from a seller if goods which were delivered in a damaged condition have been returned to the seller?

5.5   Eduservice, an educational consultancy business, ordered some data storage disks from Compusupply Limited on purchase order 53659 for the IT Department at Martley College in Broadfield. The goods were delivered to the Eduservice office at 45 The Ridings, Broadfield on 3 February.

You work in the Eduservice office as an accounts assistant. Part of your job is to deal with all the documents.

You have today (5 February 20-3) received an invoice from Compusupply. You are not happy with the service you are receiving from this company and are thinking of going elsewhere for a supplier.

Shown on the next two pages are:

•   an extract from an email from Compusupply agreeing the level of trade discount given

•   the original purchase order

•   the invoice you receive

You are to write an email to Compusupply setting out the errors that have been made. Address the email to sales@compusupply.co.uk and sign it with your own name as an accounts assistant. The date is 5 February 20-3.

Extract of email dated 1 November 20-02 from Compusupply to Eduservice

"In view of our long-standing trading relationship we are happy to increase the trade discount we allow your company from 10% to 15% from 1 November 20-2.

Kind regards

James Watts
Credit Controller
Eduservice"

EDUSERVICE	**PURCHASE ORDER**
45 The Ridings Broadfield BR2 3TR Tel 01908 333691	

TO

Compusupply Limited Unit 17 Elgar Estate, Broadfield, BR7 4ER	purchase order no 53659 date 27 January 20-3

product code	quantity	description
4573	10	Opus 100GB Storage disks @ £95 each Please deliver to: J Wales, IT Department Martley College, Fairacre, Broadfield BR5 7YT

Authorised   signature....._J Wales_...date......._27.1.20-3_..........

INVOICE

COMPUSUPPLY LIMITED
Unit 17 Elgar Estate, Broadfield, BR7 4ER
Tel 01908 765756 Fax 01908 765777 Email sales@compusupply.co.uk
VAT Reg GB 0745 4689 13

invoice to

Eduservice 45 The Ridings Broadfield BR2 3TR	

invoice no	20424
account	242
your reference	53659
date/tax point	30.01.20-3

deliver to

as above

product code	description	quantity	price	unit	total	discount %	net
4574	Opus 200GB Storage disk	10	125.00	each	125.00	10	112.50

goods total	112.50
VAT	19.68
TOTAL	132.18

terms
Net monthly
Carriage paid
E & OE

5.6 **(a)** John Smith & Co, a stationery shop, ordered 20 boxes of gel pens from Helicon Stationery Supplies on purchase order 17643 (see below).

The goods were delivered to John Smith & Co on 4 December 20-4, but the order was short by 2 boxes and only 18 boxes were delivered. This was noted in a goods received note (see the next page). The problem was advised to Helicon Supplies by email on 4 December and a credit note requested. The credit note was issued on 10 December and sent to John Smith & Co. (see the next page)

You are to check the three documents and write the text of an email from John Smith & Co to Helicon pointing out any discrepancies you find. Use your own name. The date is 12 December.

(b) John Smith & Co code all purchase invoices and credit notes with a supplier code and a general ledger code. Extracts from the two coding lists are shown below.

You are to state the supplier and general ledger codes which are to be used on the credit note on the next page.

Supplier	Supplier code
French & Co	FR002
Gemax Supplies	GE004
Helicon Stationery	HE001
JSTAT Ltd	JS001

Item	General Ledger code
Paper	5005
Pens	5010
Pension costs	5201
Power costs	7210

John Smith & Co

PURCHASE ORDER

7 Buttermere Road
Broadfield BR6 3TR
Tel 01908 761234 Fax 01908 761987
email info@johnsmith&co.co.uk
VAT REG GB 0745 8383 56

Helicon Stationery Supplies
91 High Street,
Broadfield, BR7 4ER

purchase order no   **17643**
date   **25 11 20-4**

product code	quantity	description
919BK	**20 boxes of 10**	**Gel Pens (Black)**

AUTHORISED   signature......*D Smith*..date...*25/11/20-4*

John Smith & Co

GOODS RECEIVED NOTE

GRN no.   302

supplier   Helicon Stationery Supplies

date   4 December 20-4

order ref.	quantity	description
17643	20 boxes of 10	Gel pens (black)

received by *D Patel* .... checked by ...*R T Fraser*.................

condition of goods   condition - *good*

damages - *none*

shortages √ *18 out of 20 boxes received*

CREDIT NOTE

HELICON STATIONERY SUPPLIES

91 HIGH STREET, BROADFIELD, BR7 4ER
Tel 01908 129426 Fax 01908 129919
email sales@heliconstationery.co.uk
VAT REG GB 0622 838370

to

John Smith & Co
7 Buttermere Road
Broadfield BR6 3TR

credit note no   234672
account   2984
your reference   17644
date/tax point   10 December 20-4

product code	description	quantity	price	unit	total	discount %	net
909BK	Rollerball pens (black)	3	8.00	box	24.00	10	19.20

reason for credit
Shortages

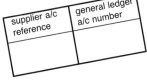

goods total	19.20
VAT @ 17.5%	3.36
TOTAL	22.56

6 Accounting for purchases and purchases returns

This chapter focuses on using the accounting system to record the details of purchases and purchases returns.

Having looked in the previous chapter at the documents and procedures involved in buying on credit we will now take the financial documents of purchases invoices and credit notes for purchases and record them in books of prime entry (day books) and in the book-keeping system of general ledger and purchases ledger.

We will be using two books of prime entry:

* purchases day book
* purchases returns day book

Information from these day books will then be transferred into the book-keeping system using accounts in general ledger and purchases ledger.

Note:

In this chapter we use the International Accounting Standards term 'payable' to mean a person who is owed money by a business; normally this is a supplier. You may also in your studies and assessments come across the traditional term 'creditor' which means exactly the same thing.

THE ACCOUNTING SYSTEM

We have seen in Chapter 1 (page 4) that the accounting system comprises a number of stages of recording and presenting financial transactions:

* financial documents
* books of prime entry (eg day books)
* double-entry book-keeping
* trial balance

In this chapter we look at how financial documents for credit purchases and purchases returns transactions are recorded in the books of prime entry, together with the entries to be made in the double-entry book-keeping accounts. Later in the book we will see how a list of the balances of the double-entry accounts is used to form the trial balance (Chapter 11).

ACCOUNTING FOR CREDIT PURCHASES AND RETURNS

In this chapter we focus on accounting for credit purchases and purchases returns transactions. Cash purchases transactions will be seen when we study the cash book (Chapter 8).

In accounting, the term 'purchases' means **the purchase of goods with the intention that they should be resold at a profit**.

This means that an office stationery shop will record as purchases those items – such as photocopier paper, ring binders – which it buys with the intention of resale at a profit. Such purchases – together with the running costs of the business, eg wages, heating and lighting, telephone – are described as **revenue expenditure**. Other asset items purchased in connection with the running of the business – eg buildings, shop fittings – are recorded not as purchases but, instead, are accounted for as the purchase of an asset, ie buildings, shop fittings – such expenditure is described as **capital expenditure**.

'Purchases returns' are when goods previously bought on credit are returned by the buyer to the supplier.

The diagram on the next page shows the order in which the accounting records are prepared for credit purchases and purchases returns transactions. You will see that the steps are:

* start with a **financial document**, either a purchases invoice or a credit note received

- enter it in the appropriate **book of prime entry** (the first accounting book in which the financial document is recorded and summarised), either purchases day book or purchases returns day book
- transfer the information from the book of prime entry into the double-entry accounts in the **general ledger**
- transfer the information from the book of prime entry into the memorandum accounts of payables (creditors) in the **purchases ledger**

accounting for credit purchases and purchases returns transactions

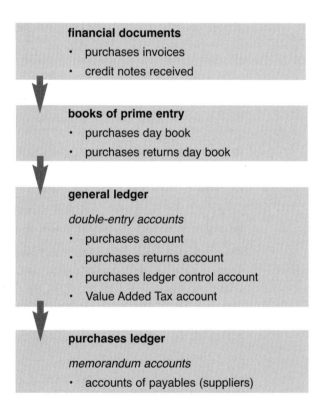

financial documents
- purchases invoices
- credit notes received

books of prime entry
- purchases day book
- purchases returns day book

general ledger

double-entry accounts
- purchases account
- purchases returns account
- purchases ledger control account
- Value Added Tax account

purchases ledger

memorandum accounts
- accounts of payables (suppliers)

We will now look in more detail at the use of the books of prime entry and the double-entry book-keeping system for credit purchases and purchases returns. These are very similar to the system already used for credit sales and sales returns in Chapter 3 and you may wish to refer to the sections of Chapter 3 which cover books of prime entry (pages 42-43), the double-entry system (pages 45-46), and methods of coding in accounting systems (page 56).

ACCOUNTING SYSTEM FOR CREDIT PURCHASES

The accounting system for credit purchases fits together in the following way:

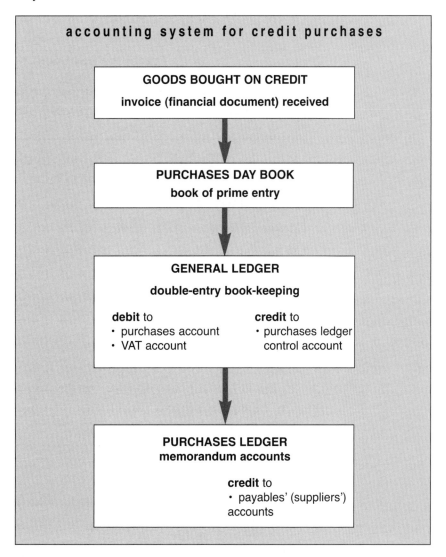

We will now look in more detail at the purchases day book and the accounting system for credit purchases.

In the examples which follow we will assume that the business is registered for Value Added Tax and that VAT is charged on invoices received from suppliers.

The VAT rate used in the examples is 17.5%.

PURCHASES DAY BOOK

The purchases day book is a collection point for accounting information on the credit purchases of a business and is set out in the following way (with sample entries shown):

Purchases Day Book						PDB57
Date	Details	Invoice number	Reference	Total	VAT*	Net
20-4				£	£	£
5 Jan	P Bond Ltd	1234	PL125	94	14	80
9 Jan	D Webster	A373	PL730	141	21	120
16 Jan	P Bond Ltd	1247	PL125	47	7	40
20 Jan	Sanders & Sons	5691	PL495	188	28	160
31 Jan	Totals for month			470	70	400
				GL2350	GL2200	GL5100

* VAT = 17.5 per cent

Notes:

- Purchases day book is prepared from financial documents – purchases invoices received from suppliers. The invoice number used is either that of the supplier's invoice (as above) or is a unique number given to each invoice by the buyer's accounts department.
- The code 'PDB57' is used for cross-referencing to the book-keeping system: here it indicates that this is page 57 of the purchases day book (PDB).
- The **reference** column (also known as the folio column) cross-references here to 'PL' – the Purchases Ledger – followed by the account number of the payable (supplier).
- The **total** column records the amount of each financial document, ie after VAT has been included.
- The code 'GL' beneath the totals amounts refers to the account numbers in General Ledger.
- Purchases day book is totalled at appropriate intervals – daily, weekly or monthly (as here) – and the total of the **net** column tells the business the amount of credit purchases for the period.

- The amounts from purchases day book are recorded in the ledger accounts.

In order to write up the purchases day book, we take purchases invoices – that have been checked and authorised – for the period and enter the details:

- date of invoice
- name of supplier
- purchase invoice number, using either the supplier's invoice number, or a unique number given to each invoice by the buyer's accounts department
- cross-reference to the supplier's account number in the purchases ledger, eg 'PL125'
- enter the total amount of the invoice into the 'total' column
- enter the VAT amount shown on the invoice – don't be concerned with any adjustments to the VAT for the effect of any settlement (cash) discounts, simply record the VAT amount shown
- enter the net amount of the invoice (often described as 'goods or services total'), before VAT is added

BOOK-KEEPING FOR CREDIT PURCHASES

After the purchases day book has been written up and totalled, the information from it is transferred to the double-entry system in general ledger. The accounts in general ledger to record the transactions from the purchases day book on the previous page are as follows:

GENERAL LEDGER

Dr	Value Added Tax Account (GL2200)		Cr
20-4	£	20-4	£
31 Jan Purchases Day Book PDB57	70		

Dr	Purchases Ledger Control Account (GL2350)		Cr
20-4	£	20-4	£
		31 Jan Purchases Day Book PDB57	470

Dr	Purchases Account (GL5100)		Cr
20-4	£	20-4	£
31 Jan Purchases Day Book PDB57	400		

Note that from the purchases day book:

- total of the total column, £470, has been credited to purchases ledger control account (which records the liability to payables)
- the total of the VAT column, £70, has been debited to VAT account (which has gained value)
- the total of the net column, £400, has been debited to purchases account (which has gained value)
- each entry in general ledger is cross-referenced back to the page number of the purchases day book; here the reference is to 'PDB57'.

The last step is to record the amount of purchases made from each individual payable (supplier). We do this by recording the purchases invoices in the purchases ledger as follows:

PURCHASES LEDGER

Dr		**P Bond Limited** (PL125)		Cr
20-4	£	20-4		£
		5 Jan	Purchases PDB57	94
		16 Jan	Purchases PDB57	47

Dr		**Sanders & Sons** (PL495)		Cr
20-4	£	20-4		£
		20 Jan	Purchases PDB57	188

Dr		**D Webster** (PL730)		Cr
20-4	£	20-4		£
		9 Jan	Purchases PDB57	141

Notes:

- the purchases day book incorporates a reference column, used to cross-reference each transaction to the personal account of each supplier in the purchases ledger (PL); this enables a particular transaction to be traced from financial document (invoice received), through the book of prime entry (purchases day book), to the supplier's account

- each entry in the purchases ledger is cross-referenced back to the page number of the purchases day book; here the reference is 'PDB57'.

memorandum accounts

The accounts in purchases ledger are prepared following the principles of double-entry book-keeping. However, they are **memorandum accounts** which means they are used to provide a note of how much each payable (supplier) is owed by the business.

Memorandum accounts are not part of double-entry but are represented in the general ledger by purchases ledger control account. This means that, here, the £470 credit entry is split up in the purchases ledger between the three suppliers' memorandum accounts. Note that memorandum accounts are often referred to as **subsidiary accounts**.

ACCOUNTING SYSTEM FOR PURCHASES RETURNS

Purchases returns (or returns out) are when goods previously bought on credit are returned by the business to its suppliers. A credit note (see page 24) is requested and, when received, it is entered in the accounting system to reduce the amount owing to the supplier.

The accounting procedures for purchases returns involve:

- **financial documents** – credit notes received from suppliers

- **book of prime entry** – purchases returns day book

- **double-entry accounts** – general ledger (purchases returns account, which records the total net amount of credit notes received, Value Added Tax account, which records the VAT amount of purchases returns, and purchases ledger control account, which records the liability to payables)

- **purchases ledger** – the memorandum accounts for each individual supplier of the business

The way in which the accounting system for purchases returns fits together is shown in the diagram on the next page.

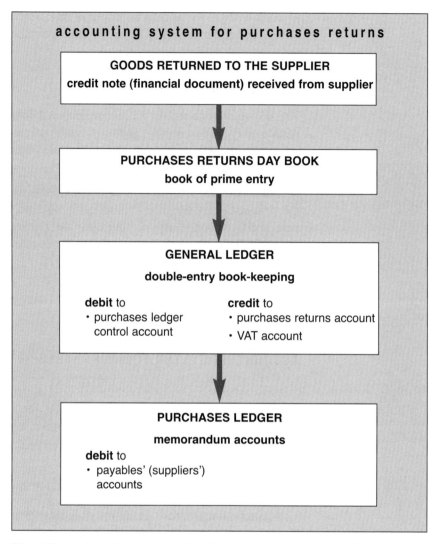

We will now look in more detail at the purchases returns day book and the double-entry accounts for purchases returns. Note that the business is registered for Value Added Tax.

PURCHASES RETURNS DAY BOOK

The purchases returns day book uses virtually the same layout as the purchases day book seen earlier in this chapter. It operates in a similar way, storing up information about purchases returns transactions until such time as a transfer is made into the double-entry accounts system. The prime documents for purchases returns day book are credit notes received from suppliers.

The purchases returns day book is written up as follows, with sample entries:

Purchases Returns Day Book					PRDB3	
Date	Details	Credit note no	Reference	Total	VAT*	Net
20-4				£	£	£
20 Jan	D Webster	123	PL730	47	7	40
27 Jan	Sanders & Sons	406	PL495	94	14	80
31 Jan	Totals for month			141	21	120
				GL2350	GL2200	GL5110

* VAT = 17.5 per cent

Notes:

- The purchases returns day book is prepared from credit notes received from suppliers. The credit note number used is either that of the supplier's credit note (as above) or is a unique number given to each credit note by the buyer's accounts department.
- The day book is totalled at appropriate intervals – weekly or monthly.
- The VAT-inclusive amounts from the total column are debited to the suppliers' individual accounts in the purchases ledger.
- The total of the VAT column is transferred to the credit of the VAT account in the general ledger.
- The total of the net column tells the business the amount of purchases returns for the period. This amount is transferred to the credit of purchases returns account in the general ledger.
- The total column records the amount of each credit note received, ie after VAT has been included. This amount is transferred to the debit of purchases ledger control account in general ledger.

BOOK-KEEPING FOR PURCHASES RETURNS

After the purchases returns day book has been written up and totalled, the information from it is transferred into the double-entry system. The accounts in the general ledger to record the transactions from the above purchases returns day book (including any other transactions already recorded on these accounts) are as follows:

GENERAL LEDGER

Dr	Value Added Tax Account (GL2200)		Cr	
20-4		£	20-4	£
31 Jan	Purchases Day Book PDB57	70	31 Jan Purchases Returns Day Book PRDB3	21

Dr	Purchases Ledger Control Account (GL2350)		Cr	
20-4		£	20-4	£
31 Jan	Purchases Returns Day Book PRDB3	141	31 Jan Purchases Day Book PDB57	470

Dr	Purchases Returns Account (GL5110)		Cr	
20-4		£	20-4	£
			31 Jan Purchases Returns Day Book PRDB3	120

The last step is to record the amount of purchases returns made to each creditor. We do this by recording the purchases returns in the memorandum accounts for each creditor in the purchases ledger as follows:

PURCHASES LEDGER

Dr	Sanders & Sons (PL495)		Cr	
20-4		£	20-4	£
27 Jan	Purchases Returns PRDB3	94	20 Jan Purchases PDB57	188

Dr	D Webster (PL730)		Cr	
20-4		£	20-4	£
20 Jan	Purchases Returns PRDB3	47	9 Jan Purchases PDB57	141

THE USE OF ANALYSED PURCHASES DAY BOOKS

Businesses use analysed day books whenever they wish to analyse purchases and purchases returns between different categories of purchases:

- goods bought for resale, often split between types of goods, eg in a clothes shop between ladies wear and mens wear
- other items of revenue expenditure, eg bills for expenses, such as telephone, electricity etc

An example of an analysed purchases day book is shown below.

Purchases Day Book									PDB86
Date	Details	Invoice	Reference	Total	VAT*	Net	Ladies wear	Mens wear	Other expenses
20-4				£	£	£	£	£	£
2 Sep	Fashions Limited	1401	PL087	141	21	120	50	70	–
4 Sep	Eastern Telephones	1402	PL061	235	35	200	–	–	200
8 Sep	Mercian Models	1403	PL102	329	49	280	280	–	–
12 Sep	Media Advertising	1404	PL092	705	105	600	–	–	600
15 Sep	Style Limited	1405	PL379	470	70	400	300	100	–
19 Sep	Wyvern Motors	1406	PL423	188	28	160	–	–	160
30 Sep	Totals for month			2,068	308	1,760	630	170	960
				GL2350	GL2200	GL5100	GL5150	GL5160	GL5190

* VAT = 17.5 per cent

Analysed purchases day books and purchases returns day books can be adapted to suit the particular needs of a business. Thus there is not a standard way in which to present the books of prime entry – the needs of the user of the information are all important. By using analysed day books, the owner of the business can see how much has been bought by departments, or categories of purchases.

Notes:

- In this purchases day book each purchases invoice has been given a unique number (starting at 1401) by the buyer's accounts department.
- The reference column is to 'PL' (Purchases Ledger) and the supplier's account number.
- The code 'GL' beneath the totals amounts refers to the account numbers in General Ledger.

- The analysis columns – here ladies wear, mens wear and other expenses – show the amount of purchases net of VAT (ie before VAT is added).
- The analysis columns analyse the net amount – by category of expenditure – from purchases invoices.

Case Study

1.850

1.600

WYVERN TRADERS – PURCHASES AND RETURNS

To bring together the material covered in this chapter, we will look at a comprehensive Case Study which makes use of

- **books of prime entry**
  - purchases day book
  - purchases returns day book
- **general ledger accounts**
  - purchases account
  - purchases ledger control account
  - Value Added Tax account
- **purchases ledger accounts**
  - creditors' memorandum accounts

The Chapter Summary (pages 123 and 124) includes diagrams which summarise the procedures for recording credit purchases and purchases returns transactions in the accounting system.

situation

Wyvern Traders is a wholesaler of stationery and office equipment. The business is registered for VAT. The following are the credit purchases and purchases returns transactions for April 20-4:

20-4		
1 Apr	Purchased goods from Midland Supplies, £120.00 + VAT, their invoice no 12486	
9 Apr	Returned goods to Midland Supplies, £40.00 + VAT, credit note no 104 received	
14 Apr	Purchased goods from Swan Equipment, £80.00 + VAT, their invoice no P076	
28 Apr	Purchased goods from Swan Equipment, £160.00 + VAT, their invoice no P102	
30 Apr	Returned goods to Swan Equipment, £80.00 + VAT, credit note no X102 received	

The day books, general ledger and purchases ledger accounts are illustrated on the next two pages: arrows indicate the transfers from the day books to the individual accounts. Note that some accounts have been repeated on both pages in order to show, on the same page, the accounts relating to a particular day book: in practice a business would keep all the transactions together in one account.

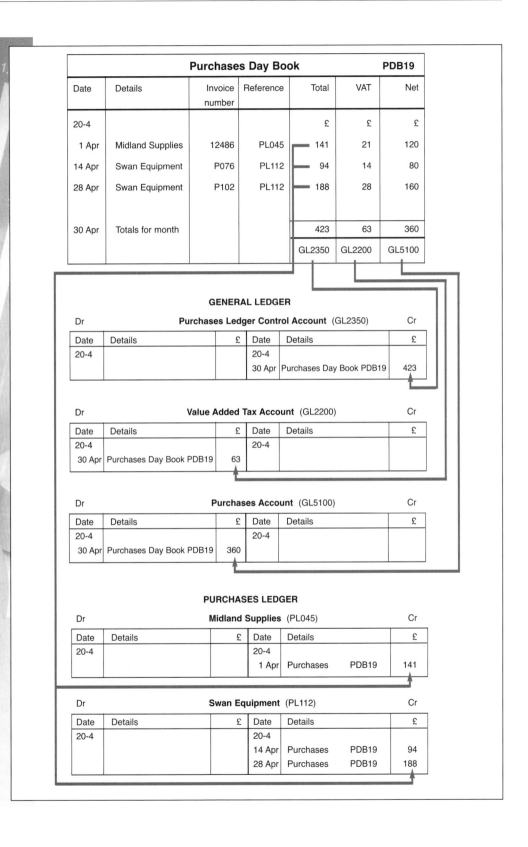

Purchases Day Book | | | | | | **PDB19**

Date	Details	Invoice number	Reference	Total	VAT	Net
20-4				£	£	£
1 Apr	Midland Supplies	12486	PL045	141	21	120
14 Apr	Swan Equipment	P076	PL112	94	14	80
28 Apr	Swan Equipment	P102	PL112	188	28	160
30 Apr	Totals for month			423	63	360
				GL2350	GL2200	GL5100

GENERAL LEDGER

Dr   **Purchases Ledger Control Account** (GL2350)   Cr

Date	Details	£	Date	Details	£
20-4			20-4		
			30 Apr	Purchases Day Book PDB19	423

Dr   **Value Added Tax Account** (GL2200)   Cr

Date	Details	£	Date	Details	£
20-4			20-4		
30 Apr	Purchases Day Book PDB19	63			

Dr   **Purchases Account** (GL5100)   Cr

Date	Details	£	Date	Details	£
20-4			20-4		
30 Apr	Purchases Day Book PDB19	360			

PURCHASES LEDGER

Dr   **Midland Supplies** (PL045)   Cr

Date	Details	£	Date	Details		£
20-4			20-4			
			1 Apr	Purchases	PDB19	141

Dr   **Swan Equipment** (PL112)   Cr

Date	Details	£	Date	Details		£
20-4			20-4			
			14 Apr	Purchases	PDB19	94
			28 Apr	Purchases	PDB19	188

Purchases Returns Day Book — PRDB7

Date	Details	Credit note number	Reference	Total	VAT	Net
20-4				£	£	£
9 Apr	Midland Supplies	104	PL045	47	7	40
30 Apr	Swan Equipment	X102	PL112	94	14	80
30 Apr	Totals for month			141	21	120
				GL2350	GL2200	GL5110

GENERAL LEDGER

Dr   **Purchases Ledger Control Account** (GL2350)   Cr

Date	Details	£	Date	Details	£
20-4			20-4		
30 Apr	Purchases Returns Day Book PRDB7	141	30 Apr	Purchases Day Book PDB19	*423

Dr   **Value Added Tax Account** (GL2200)   Cr

Date	Details	£	Date	Details	£
20-4			20-4		
30 Apr	Purchases Day Book PDB19	*63	30 Apr	Purchases Returns Day Book PRDB7	21

Dr   **Purchases Returns Account** (GL5110)   Cr

Date	Details	£	Date	Details	£
20-4			20-4		
			30 Apr	Purchases Returns Day Book PRDB7	120

PURCHASES LEDGER

Dr   **Midland Supplies** (PL045)   Cr

Date	Details	£	Date	Details	£
20-4			20-4		
9 Apr	Purchases Returns PRDB7	47	1 Apr	Purchases PDB19	*141

Dr   **Swan Equipment** (PL112)   Cr

Date	Details	£	Date	Details	£
20-4			20-4		
30 Apr	Purchases Returns PRDB7	94	14 Apr	Purchases PDB19	*94
			28 Apr	Purchases PDB19	*188

* transactions entered previously

Chapter Summary

The diagrams on the next two pages summarise the material we have studied in this chapter. They shows the procedures for recording transactions in the accounting system for credit purchases and purchases returns.

Further chapter summary points follow on page 125.

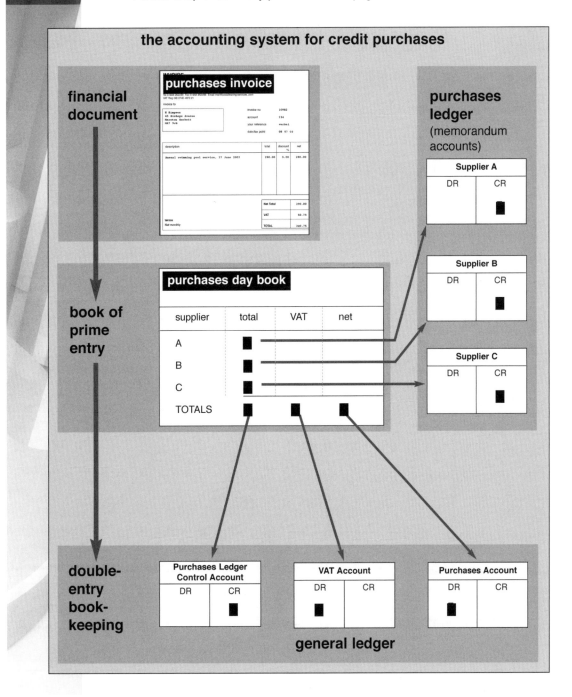

Chapter
Summary

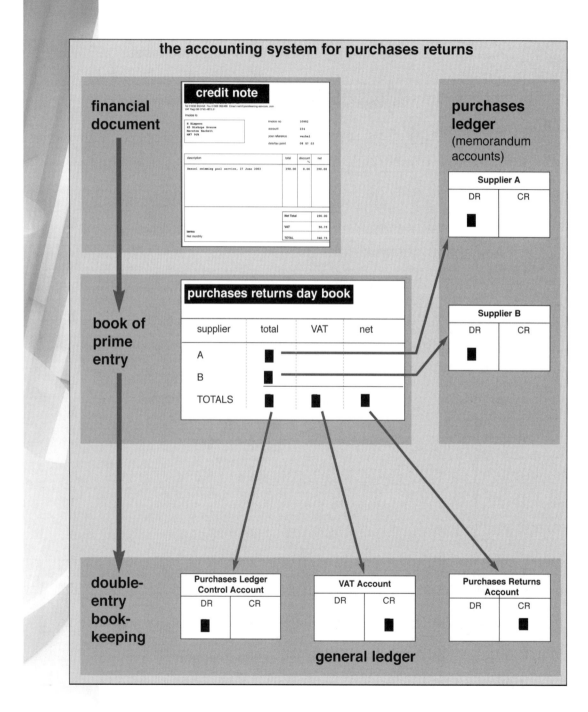

■   The accounting system comprises a number of specific stages of recording and presenting financial transactions:

    – financial documents

    – books of prime entry (eg day books)

    – double-entry book-keeping

    – trial balance

■   The financial documents relating to credit purchases are:

    – purchases invoices

    – credit notes received

■   Purchases day book is the book of prime entry for credit purchases. It is prepared from purchases invoices received from suppliers.

■   Purchases returns day book is the book of prime entry for purchases returns. It is prepared from credit notes received from suppliers.

■   Analysed purchases and purchases returns day books are used when a business wishes to analyse its purchases between different categories of expenditure.

■   Recording credit purchases in the double-entry system uses:

    – financial documents, purchases invoices

    – book of prime entry, purchases day book

    – double-entry accounts in the general ledger

    – memorandum accounts in the purchases ledger

■   Recording purchases returns in the double-entry system uses:

    – financial documents, credit notes received from suppliers

    – book of prime entry, purchases returns day book

    – double-entry accounts in the general ledger

    – memorandum accounts in the purchases ledger

Key Terms

purchases	the purchase of goods with the intention that they should be resold at a profit
revenue expenditure	the cost of purchases and running costs of the business
capital expenditure	the cost of asset items other than for resale, purchased in connection with the running of the business, eg buildings, shop fittings
purchases day book	book of prime entry prepared from purchases invoices
purchases returns	goods purchased on credit which are returned to the supplier
purchases returns day book	book of prime entry prepared from credit notes received from suppliers
analysed day books	day books which incorporate analysis columns, for example between – goods bought for resale, often split between different types of goods – other items of revenue expenditure
general ledger	ledger section which includes – purchases account – purchases returns account – purchases ledger control account – Value Added Tax account
purchases ledger	subsidiary ledger section which contains the memorandum accounts of the firm's payables (suppliers)
memorandum account	a subsidiary ledger (eg purchases ledger) account which provides a note of individual amounts (eg owing by the business to suppliers)

Activities

6.1   Which one of the following is a book of prime entry?

(a)   purchases account

(b)   Value Added Tax account

(c)   purchases returns day book

(d)   purchases ledger account of M Ostrowski

Answer (a) or (b) or (c) or (d)

6.2   Which one of the following is in the right order?

(a)   purchases returns day book; purchases ledger control account; credit note issued; purchases returns account; supplier's account

(b)   purchases returns account; supplier's account; purchases ledger control account; purchases returns day book; credit note issued

(c)   purchases returns day book; purchases returns account; purchases ledger control account; supplier's account; credit note issued

(d)   credit note issued; purchases returns day book; purchases returns account; purchases ledger control account; supplier's account

Answer (a) or (b) or (c) or (d)

6.3   Which one of the following are the correct general ledger entries for a purchases returns transaction?

(a)   debit purchases ledger control; debit VAT; credit purchases returns

(b)   debit purchases ledger control; credit purchases returns; credit VAT

(c)   debit purchases returns; debit VAT; credit purchases ledger control

(d)   debit purchases returns; credit purchases ledger control; credit VAT

Answer (a) or (b) or (c) or (d)

6.4   Explain in note format:

(a)   the principles of recording a credit purchases transaction in the accounting system

(b)   the principles of recording a purchases returns transaction in the accounting system

For Activities 6.5 and 6.6:

- work in pounds and pence, where appropriate
- the rate of Value Added Tax is to be calculated at 17.5% (when calculating VAT amounts, you should ignore fractions of a penny, ie round down to a whole penny)
- use a coding system incorporating the following:

purchases day book	– PDB36
purchases returns day book	– PRDB11

		general ledger account numbers	
		purchases ledger control account	– GL2350
purchases ledger account numbers		purchases account	– GL5100
AMC Enterprises	– PL520	purchases returns account	– GL5110
S Green	– PL574	Value Added Tax account	– GL2200
I Johnstone	– PL604		
Mercia Manufacturing	– PL627		
L Murphy	– PL659		
Severn Supplies	– PL721		

6.5 During April 20-5, Wyvern Wholesalers had the following credit transactions:

20-5

2 Apr	Purchased goods from Severn Supplies £250 + VAT, invoice no 6789
5 Apr	Purchased goods from I Johnstone £210 + VAT, invoice no A241
9 Apr	Purchased goods from L Murphy £185 + VAT, invoice no 2456
15 Apr	Purchased goods from Mercia Manufacturing £180 + VAT, invoice no X457
19 Apr	Purchased goods from AMC Enterprises £345 + VAT, invoice no AMC 456
26 Apr	Purchased goods from S Green £395 + VAT, invoice no 2846

You are to:

(a) Enter the above transactions in Wyvern Wholesaler's purchases day book for April 20-5.

(b) Record the accounting entries in Wyvern Wholesaler's general ledger and purchases ledger.

(Note that you will need to retain these ledger accounts for use with Activity 6.6)

6.6 The following are the purchases returns of Wyvern Wholesalers for April 20-5. They are to be:

(a) entered in the purchases returns day book for April 20-5

(b) recorded in the general ledger and purchases ledger (use the ledgers already prepared in the answer to Activity 6.5)

20-5

7 Apr	Returned goods to Severn Supplies £50 + VAT, credit note no 225 received
14 Apr	Returned goods to L Murphy £80 + VAT, credit note no X456 received
21 Apr	Returned goods to AMC Enterprises £125 + VAT, credit note no 3921 received
29 Apr	Returned goods to S Green £68 + VAT, credit note no SG247 received

6.7 You are employed by Hussein Limited as a book-keeper. The business has a manual accounting system. Double-entry takes place in the general ledger; individual accounts of creditors are kept as memorandum accounts in the purchases ledger. The VAT rate is 17.5%.

Notes:

- show your answer with a tick, words or figures, as appropriate
- coding is not required

(a) The following transactions all took place on 30 April 20-4 and have been entered into the purchases day book as shown below. No entries have yet been made into the ledger system.

Purchases day book

Date 20-4	Details	Invoice number	Total £	VAT £	Net £
30 April	Seng Ltd	4517	1,128	168	960
30 April	Peall & Co	2384	2,773	413	2,360
30 April	Knightons	A761	4,089	609	3,480
30 April	Galeazzi plc	7248	1,457	217	1,240
	Totals		9,447	1,407	8,040

What will be the entries in the general ledger?

General ledger

Account name	Amount £	Debit ✓	Credit ✓

What will be the entries in the purchases ledger?

Purchases ledger

Account name	Amount £	Debit ✓	Credit ✓

(b) The following transactions all took place on 30 April 20-4 and have been entered into the purchases returns day book as shown below. No entries have yet been made into the ledger system.

Purchases returns day book

Date 20-4	Details	Credit note number	Total £	VAT £	Net £
30 April	Martin & Co	381	1,034	154	880
30 April	Wentworth Stores	C48	658	98	560
	Totals		1,692	252	1,440

What will be the entries in the general ledger?

General ledger

Account name	Amount £	Debit ✓	Credit ✓

What will be the entries in the purchases ledger?

Purchases ledger

Account name	Amount £	Debit ✓	Credit ✓

6.8   The following is taken from the coding lists used at a business called Fashion Trading.

Supplier	Purchases ledger account code
Bingham Fashions	BIN001
Bourne Stores	BOU002
Elite Trading	ELI001
Green Dragon	GRE001
Guest & Co	GUE002
High Society	HIG001
Modes Ltd	MOD001
Myers Trading	MYE002
Treetop Stores	TRE001
Wragby Ltd	WRA001
Zeta & Co	ZET001

You are to set up the purchases ledger account codes for the new suppliers shown below.

Supplier	Purchases ledger account code
Bridon Ltd	
Foster & Co	
Hirst & Co	

7 Prepare payments to suppliers

this chapter covers...

In Chapter 5 'Processing documents from suppliers' we described the financial documents dealt with by a purchaser of goods and services on credit. These documents included the purchase invoice, credit note, delivery note and goods received note.

In this chapter we describe the next stage in the process – the preparation of the documentation needed when payment is to be made for the goods or services purchased.

The chapter covers the following areas:

- *a brief review of the purchasing process*

- *checking a statement of account received from a supplier against the transactions in the account of the supplier in the purchases ledger*

- *identifying any discrepancies between a statement of account and transactions in the account of the supplier in the purchases ledger*

- *calculating the amount due to each supplier on the correct payment date*

- *preparing remittance advices for making payment by cheque or through BACS, the bank computer direct payment system*

This chapter will not go into detail about the various bank payment systems. These are fully explained elsewhere.

A REVIEW OF THE PURCHASING PROCESS

When a business makes a purchase of goods on credit it deals with a number of financial documents. These were covered in Chapter 5 and include:

- **purchase order** – issued by the buyer ordering the goods
- **delivery note** – sent with the goods by the supplier
- **goods received note** – details of goods received and any discrepancies
- **purchase invoice** – received from the supplier, setting out what is owed
- **purchase credit note** – any refund to the buyer's account for missing, damaged or incorrect goods or any mistakes on the invoice

The next stage – dealt with in this chapter – is:

- the receipt of the supplier's **statement of account** setting out what is owed – the transactions on the statement should be checked with the supplier's account in the purchases ledger of the buyer
- the preparation of a **remittance advice** by the buyer, advising the supplier that payment is being made

This stage, and its place in the process, is shown at the bottom of the diagram below.

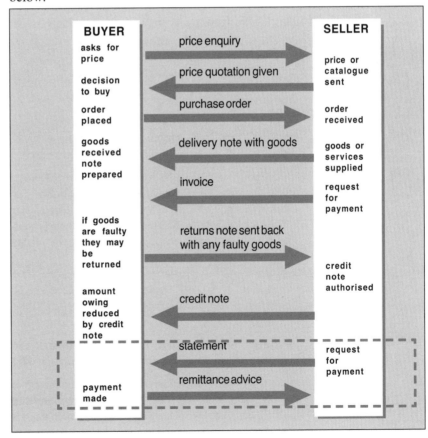

RECONCILING THE SUPPLIER STATEMENT OF ACCOUNT

Chapter 5 described the processes of checking all the purchases documentation to identify and deal with any discrepancies. The documents involved are:

- the delivery note and the actual goods received (possibly using a goods received note)
- the supplier invoices and credit notes for calculation errors
- the supplier invoices and credit notes against the purchase order

By the time that all these checks have been made and the invoices and credit notes have been authorised, the buyer should settle up the **supplier's account in the purchases ledger**. This account should contain details of all the transactions such as payments, purchases and purchases returns. The account should in fact mirror all the items which will appear in the supplier's **statement of account**. See the next page for an example of a statement of account and the supplier account in the purchases ledger. Compare the two. This process is known as **reconciliation**, which basically means 'tying up' the transactions.

This is all illustrated in the Case Study which follows.

Case Study

1.850

1.600

KNITWICK – SUPPLIER STATEMENT RECONCILIATION

situation

Knitwick Traders is a clothing company which specialises in fashion wear. It has a regular trading relationship with Medici Importers which supplies it with high quality Italian clothes.

Medici Importers sends statements of account to Knitwick at the end of each month and Knitwick normally settles the account at the beginning of the next month. During the month of November 20-5 the following documents were sent to Knitwick by Medici Importers. They were checked by Knitwick and were found to be correct.

2 invoices:	8 November	Ref 4312	£850.00
	14 November	Ref 4367	£120.00
1 credit note:	20 November	Ref 534	£85.00

In addition, Knitwick sent £674.50 in settlement of October's account to Medici Importer's bank account through the BACS system in the first week of November.

In the first week of December, Knitwick received the statement of account shown on the next page. You have been asked to reconcile the statement with the purchases ledger account for Medici Importers also shown on the next page.

STATEMENT OF ACCOUNT

MEDICI IMPORTERS

8 San Marco Avenue, Broadfield, BR2 8DC
Tel 01908 765101 Fax 01908 765109 Email info@medicimporters.co.uk
VAT REG GB 0532 4672 21

TO

Knitwick Traders
Unit 14 Landseer Estate
Hull
HU9 6CV

account   2894

date   30 11 20-5

date	details	debit £		credit £		balance £
01 11 20-5	Balance b/f	674.50	✓			674.50
05 11 20-5	BACS payment			674.50	✓	00.00
08 11 20-5	Invoice 4312	850.00	✓			850.00
14 11 20-5	Invoice 4367	120.00	✓			970.00
20 11 20-5	Credit note 534			85.00	✓	885.00
				TOTAL		**885.00**

Debit	Purchases Ledger: Medici Importers Account					Credit		
20-5	**Details**	**£**	**p**	**20-5**	**Details**		**£**	**p**
5 Nov	Bank	✓ 674	50	1 Nov	Balance b/d	✓	674	50
20 Nov	Purchases returns	✓ 85	00	8 Nov	Purchases	✓	850	00
				14 Nov	Purchases	✓	120	00

solution

Knitwick will compare the two documents and tick off the items which appear in both documents. These are shown here in the two different grey boxes for purposes of illustration only.

All the transactions are accounted for – there are no unticked amounts which might indicate some form of discrepancy.

This means that the two documents have now been 'reconciled' – ie they both tie up with each other and payment of the account – the £885.00 owing – will be authorised and made on the due date.

DEALING WITH DISCREPANCIES

The Case Study on the previous two pages has shown a situation where all the documentation is correct and has been reconciled; all is well and payment can then be authorised and paid on the due date.

It is assumed here that the relevant financial documents – eg invoices and credit notes – have already been checked for accuracy and are free from any discrepancies.

But there may sometimes be discrepancies between the **supplier's statement of account** and the supplier's account kept in the buyer's **purchases ledger**. These will need to be sorted out before payment can be made.

These problems may be sorted out at accounts assistant level, or if the problem is more serious, by a line manager. Examples include:

- **an invoice or credit note which appears on the supplier's statement, but for the wrong amount**

  – the document will be held by the buyer and the amount can be verified, so this is likely to be an error made by the supplier when entering the amount in the accounts; it will need to be queried by the buyer and investigated and put right by the supplier

- **an invoice or credit note is on the supplier's statement and not in the buyer's purchases ledger**

  – this could be an invoice or credit note not posted to the buyer's purchases ledger, or to the wrong supplier's account, by the buyer; this should be investigated and if there is an error by the buyer, included in the payment of account

- **an invoice or credit note is in the buyer's purchases ledger and not on the supplier's statement**

  – this could be an invoice or credit note not posted to the supplier's accounts, or posted to the wrong customer account by the supplier; this item should be queried by the buyer and, if there is an error made by the supplier, included in the payment of account

- **an invoice or credit note which appears twice on the supplier's statement**

  – this is an obvious duplication of an invoice or credit note by the supplier (it does happen!); the supplier should be notified of the error and the amount not included in the payment of account

The lesson here is that accurate reconciliation of the supplier statement and purchases ledger account is very important: if a payment is made and there is an undetected discrepancy, it can be very difficult to put things right.

INVOICE AUTHORISATION AND DISPUTED INVOICES

statement or no statement?

It has been assumed in this chapter so far that suppliers will send out statements as a matter of course.

If statements are issued, businesses generally pay regularly on receipt of the statement, as this is an easier way of calculating payment. This is the situation set out in the Case Study earlier in this chapter (see pages 134-135).

In commercial practice, however, **statements are not always sent out by suppliers**. They rely instead on each customer making payment of invoices when they are due, adjusting for any credit notes issued.

Whatever method is used by a buyer for sorting out the payment of the account, certain principles remain the same:

- invoices should be paid by the due date, which can be calculated from the terms of the invoice
- invoices should be **checked** and **authorised** before the payment date

invoice authorisation

In most organisations invoices that have been checked are passed to the person in the Accounts Department who deals with making payments to suppliers. These invoices will then have to be **authorised** for payment.

When an invoice is checked and found to be correct, the person carrying out the check will usually mark the document and authorise it for payment. This authorisation can take a number of forms:

- the checker can initial and date the invoice, and tick it or write 'pay' as an authorisation
- the organisation may have a special rubber stamp which can be used in the authorisation process – this stamp may also allow provide space for **coding**, eg the cost code (the account number for the type of expense) and the purchase order reference number which can be entered in the purchases day book and also used for internal filing purposes; it may also contain the signature or initials of the person who has authority to authorise the invoice for payment

This procedure of authorisation helps the efficiency of the organisation:

- the checker's initials will be there in case of any future query on the invoice, eg an undetected error
- the invoice will be in the system for payment on the due date

disputed invoices

In this chapter so far we have assumed that a business

- will pay the total amount shown on the statement
- will pay all the invoices that are due and authorised for payment

There are times, however, when a business might decide that an invoice on a statement should not be paid. Normally in an accounts office you will be able to see this on the statement because the invoice will not be ticked, or you may get a note from your line manager telling you not to pay certain items. The invoice may be **disputed** with the supplier: for example, your business may claim that the goods supplied are incorrect while the supplier states that the wrong goods were ordered in the first place.

Now read the following Case Study which explains how to calculate a payment which involves a disputed invoice.

Case Study

ALDERSGATE SUPPLIES – PAYMENT OF ACCOUNT

situation

You work in the Accounts Department of Krumm & Co which is supplied with electrical equipment by Aldersgate Supplies.

It is your job to prepare the payments for all suppliers at the beginning of each month. The latest statement from Aldersgate Supplies is shown on the next page and an email dated 4 December from your supervisor is set out below.

The ticks on the statement indicate the items that are recorded in the purchases ledger and will have to be taken into account when payment is made.

email	
from	henry@krumm.co.uk
subject	Aldersgate Supplies account - disputed invoice
date	4 December 20-5 12:01:11 GMT
to	a.student@krumm.co.uk

Hi Aslam

Please note that Invoice 16700 for £450 is in dispute. Aldersgate clearly misread our purchase order and sent the wrong equipment, but still claim that they sent us the right stuff. On no account should this invoice be paid until the dispute is settled. Thanks.

Regards
Henry

STATEMENT OF ACCOUNT
ALDERSGATE SUPPLIES

10 Aldersgate Street, London EC1A 7GH
Tel 0207 7051017 Fax 0207 7051231 Email sales@aldersgatesupplies.co.uk
VAT REG GB 6733 8372 99

TO

Krumm & Co
56 Eccles Road
Bolton
BL7 4DF

account   26742

date   30 11 20-5

date	details	debit £	credit £	balance £
01 11 20-5	Balance b/f	1250.70 ✓		1250.70
04 11 20-5	BACS payment		1250.70 ✓	00.00
08 11 20-5	Invoice 16700	450.00		450.00
14 11 20-5	Invoice 16810	790.00 ✓		1240.00
20 11 20-5	Credit note 534		79.00 ✓	1161.00
27 11 20-5	Invoice 16985	800.00 ✓		1961.00

TOTAL	1961.00

solution

The payment amount is worked out as follows:

calculation (£)

1   The first two items represent the balance outstanding at the beginning of November and then the payment made by Krumm & Co. They are the same amount (a debit and a credit) and therefore cancel each other out.

0

2   Invoice 16700 for £450 is in dispute and so is not included

0

3   Invoice 16810 for £790 is added on

+ 790.00

4   Credit note 534 for £79 is deducted

– 79.00

5   Invoice 16985 for £800 is added on

+ 800.00

The total payment to be made to Aldersgate Supplies is £1511

= £1511.00

The next step is to prepare a remittance advice note to advise Aldersgate Supplies of the payment being made through the banking system.

PREPARING REMITTANCE ADVICES

definition

As we saw in Chapter 5, a **remittance advice** is a note which can be posted, faxed or emailed, stating that a certain amount of money has been sent by a credit customer to a supplier in settlement of an account. A remittance advice is used:

- **to accompany a cheque** – a practice which will decrease in use as the cheque is gradually phased out as a form of payment in the UK, or
- to advise the sending of a payment **direct to the seller's bank account** through **BACS**, the bank computer payment transfer system

completing the remittance advice

A remittance advice normally takes one of two forms:

- **a list of all the items which make up the payment**

  This is very useful for the supplier as it will enable the supplier's accounts department to reconcile the incoming payment with the customer's account in the sales ledger by ticking off all the items. Sometimes, if the account is very active and a computer accounting system is used, the remittance advice may contain hundreds of items and take up a number of pages. To make things simple in this text and in your studies, remittance advices are normally restricted to just a few items.

- **notification of the total amount**

  This is the simplest form of remittance advice: it just sets out the fact that a payment for a certain amount is being made by cheque or by BACS.

A cheque remittance advice listing individual transactions is shown below.

An explanation of the details that have to be completed on a BACS remittance advice is given on the next page, continuing the Case Study.

TO	REMITTANCE ADVICE	FROM
Cool Socks Limited Unit 45 Elgar Estate, Broadfield, BR7 4ER	8 November 20-3	**Vogue Ltd** **56 Shaftesbury Road** **Manorfield** **MA1 6GP**

date	your reference	our reference	payment amount
03 11 20-3	INVOICE 788106	876213	500.00
15 11 20-3	INVOICE 788256	876287	220.10
20 11 20-3	CREDIT NOTE 12218	876287	(22.01)
		CHEQUE TOTAL	698.09

Case Study

1.850

ALDERSGATE SUPPLIES – REMITTANCE ADVICE

situation – continued

You work in the Accounts Department of Krumm & Co which has a supplier, Aldersgate Supplies. You are asked to complete the remittance advice advising that a BACS payment is being sent direct to the bank account of Aldersgate Supplies.

solution

The completed document is shown below.

BACS REMITTANCE ADVICE

FROM:
Krumm & Co
56 Eccles Road
Bolton BL7 4DF

TO
Aldersgate Supplies **1**
10 Aldersgate Street, London EC1A 7GH

03 12 20-5 **2**

date **3**	your reference **4**	our reference **5**	payment amount £ **6**
17 11 20-5	Invoice 16810	PO98756	790.00
24 11 20-5	Credit note 534	PO98756	(79.00)
30 11 20-5	Invoice 16985	PO98792	800.00
		TOTAL	1511.00 **7**

8
THIS AMOUNT HAS BEEN PAID BY BACS CREDIT TRANSFER DIRECTLY INTO YOUR BANK ACCOUNT AT HRBC BANK ACCOUNT NO 79001875 SORT CODE 41 22 01

The following details have been completed by Krumm & Co:

1   at the top left, the name and address of the supplier – Aldersgate Supplies

2   at the top right, the date of the transfer of the money – 3 December 20-5

3   'date' – the dates of each of the documents listed

4   'your reference' – the description and supplier reference numbers of the invoices and credit note listed

5   'our reference' – Krumm & Co's purchase order numbers relating to the listed documents

6   'payment amount' – the amounts of the invoices and the credit note; note that the credit note amount is in brackets because it is deducted and not added

7   'total' – the amount being transferred to Aldersgate Supplies' bank account

8   at the bottom – details of the bank account number and sort code number of Aldersgate Supplies' bank (HRBC)

Chapter Summary

- When a business ordering goods on credit from a supplier has checked all the financial documents – invoice, delivery note, credit note – it will then be in a position to settle up the supplier's account in the purchases ledger.

- A common practice is for the supplier to send a **statement of account** to each customer, listing all the transactions – sales, returns, payments – which will then be recorded in the **purchases ledger account**.

- It is important that the customer checks that the items on the supplier's statement of account 'tie up' with the items in the supplier's account in the purchases ledger. This process is known as a **reconciliation**.

- If there are any **discrepancies** between the supplier's statement of account and the purchases ledger account they must be identified and investigated. They will affect the amount of money that will be paid to the supplier.

- When payment of the account is made by the buyer, the amount is calculated by totalling **authorised invoices** due for payment and deducting any **authorised credit notes** and **discrepancies** that have been found.

- Payment on the due date is advised to the supplier by completing and sending a **remittance advice**, either with a cheque or with details of a BACS payment made direct to the bank account of the supplier.

Key Terms

statement of account
document issued by a supplier listing all the payments, invoices and credit notes on the account, providing a total of the amount due

purchases ledger account
the account of the supplier in the accounting records of the buyer; it will also list the transactions on the account

reconciliation
a comparison and 'tying up' of transactions in two documents – in this case the statement of account and purchase ledger – in order to check for any discrepancies

discrepancy
a difference between the transactions recorded in two separate documents – for example a wrong figure highlighting an error or even a 'wrong' document such as a disputed invoice

remittance advice
an advice sent to a supplier advising the sending of an amount of money, either by cheque or direct to the supplier's account through the banking system

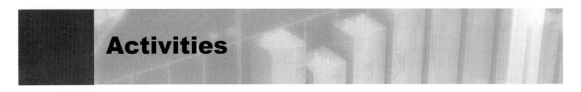

Activities

7.1   The two documents that have to be reconciled to work out the amount owing to a supplier are:

(a)   the invoice and the remittance advice

(b)   the supplier statement and the remittance advice

(c)   the supplier statement and the supplier's purchases ledger account in the books of the buyer

(d)   the remittance advice and the supplier's purchases ledger account in the books of the buyer

State which one of these four options is the correct answer.

7.2   The following must be checked and authorised for payment before a supplier payment can be prepared by a business that has received goods on credit terms:

(a)   supplier invoice

(b)   delivery note

(c)   remittance advice

(d)   supplier account in the purchases ledger

State which one of these four options is the correct answer.

7.3   If you found two purchases invoices for £250 with the same date and invoice number listed in a supplier statement you would need to query it and:

(a)   add £250 to the amount owing to the supplier as shown on the statement

(b)   deduct £250 from the amount owing to the supplier as shown on the statement

(c)   enter the invoice amount in the supplier's account in the purchases ledger

(d)   pay the total amount owing as shown on the supplier statement

State which one of these four options is the correct answer.

7.4   A remittance advice is used:

(a)   instead of a cheque when paying a supplier

(b)   instead of a BACS payment when paying a supplier

(c)   to accompany a cheque when paying a supplier

(d)   to request payment when returning goods

State which one of these four options is the correct answer.

7.5 You work in the Accounts Department of Hemsley Ltd. One of your routine tasks is to reconcile the supplier statements of account with the supplier accounts in the purchases ledger.

You are to reconcile the statement of account and purchases ledger account of your supplier Luxon Traders shown below. If you find any discrepancies:

· explain what the error could be

· suggest what you would do to resolve the problem

· state the amount you think the payment should be

STATEMENT OF ACCOUNT

LUXON TRADERS

56 High Street, Fowey, Cornwall, TR4 9DS

info@luxontraders.co.uk

TO

| Hemsley Limited |
| 6 Enterprise Park |
| Luton |
| LU7 3BN |

account   9133

date   31 03 20-1

date	details	debit £	credit £	balance £
01 03 20-1	Balance b/f	156.00		156.00
05 03 20-1	BACS payment		156.00	00.00
08 03 20-1	Invoice 76333	150.00		150.00
08 03 20-1	Invoice 76333	150.00		300.00
20 03 20-1	Credit note 923		50.00	250.00
	TOTAL			250.00

Debit	Purchases Ledger: Luxon Traders Account						Credit	
20-1	Details	£	p	20-1	Details	£	p
5 Mar	Bank	156	00	1 Mar	Balance b/d	156	00
20 Mar	Purchases returns	50	00	8 Mar	Purchases	150	00

7.6 You work in the Accounts Department of R J Powell Ltd. One of your routine tasks is to reconcile the supplier statements of account with the supplier accounts in the purchases ledger.

You are to reconcile the statement of account and purchases ledger account of your supplier A Krauss Limited shown below. If you find any discrepancies:

- explain what the error could be

- suggest what you would do to resolve the problem

- state the amount you think the payment should be

STATEMENT OF ACCOUNT

A Krauss Limited

213 Farringdon Road, Latcham, LA4 5FG
sales@akrausstrading.co.uk

TO

R J Powell Limited
48,Heathside Street
Broadheath
WR2 8NB

account   32123

date   30 04 20-1

date	details	debit £	credit £	balance £
01 04 20-1	Balance b/f	990.00		990.00
07 04 20-1	BACS payment		990.00	00.00
09 04 20-1	Invoice 12856	233.25		233.25
19 04 20-1	Invoice 12932	109.50		342.75
			TOTAL	342.75

Debit	Purchases Ledger: A Krauss Limited Account					Credit		
20-1	**Details**	**£**	**p**	**20-1**	**Details**	**£**	**p**
7 Apr	Bank	990	00	1 Apr	Balance b/d	990	00
22 Apr	Purchases returns	72	90	9 Apr	Purchases	233	25
				19 Apr	Purchases	109	50

7.7 Complete the remittance advice on the bottom of the page, using the details and the ticked items on the statement shown below. The purchase order number for the invoices are PO85262 and PO85271 and for credit note PO85248. The bank details are on the advice. The date is 3 October.

STATEMENT OF ACCOUNT
ALDERSGATE SUPPLIES

10 Aldersgate Street, London EC1A 7GH
Tel 0207 7051017 Fax   0207 7051231 Email sales@aldersgatesupplies.co.uk
VAT REG GB 6733 8372 99

TO

Hetherington Limited
Unit 23 Wessex Estate
Langborne Road
Seatown SE8 5VZ

account   26742

date   30 09 20-5

date	details	debit £	credit £	balance £
01 09 20-5	Balance b/f	550.00 ✓		550.00
04 09 20-5	BACS payment		550.00 ✓	00.00
08 09 20-5	Invoice 10945	120.75 ✓		120.75
14 09 20-5	Invoice 10963	380.25 ✓		501.00
20 09 20-5	Credit note 109		46.00 ✓	455.00
			TOTAL	455.00

BACS REMITTANCE ADVICE

FROM:
Hetherington Limited
Unit 23 Wessex Estate
Langborne Road
Seatown SE8 5VZ

TO

date:

date	your reference	our reference	payment amount £

TOTAL

THIS AMOUNT HAS BEEN PAID BY BACS CREDIT TRANSFER DIRECTLY INTO YOUR BANK ACCOUNT AT ALBION BANK ACCOUNT NO 17643987 SORT CODE 97 43 83

7.8   Hetherington Limited also sends out cheques with some remittance advices.

Complete the cheque remittance advice and cheque set out below. You should not sign the cheque as only a director has authority to do so. The settlement details are as follows:

Date: 5 June 20-5

Supplier: Sutherland & Co, 67 Great March Street, Eastwick, EA3 9JN

Invoice 7856 for £345.90 dated 23 May 20-5, purchase order 472984

Credit note 4562 for £87.50 dated 29 May 20-5, purchase order 472975

REMITTANCE ADVICE

TO

FROM:
Hetherington Limited
Unit 23 Wessex Estate
Langborne Road
Seatown SE8 5VZ

date:

date	your reference	our reference	payment amount £

CHEQUE TOTAL

Southern Bank PLC
Mereford Branch
16 Broad Street, Mereford MR1 7TR

date

97-76-54

Pay

only

Account payee only

£

HETHERINGTON LTD

123456   97 76 54   68384939

Director

8 Cash book

In this chapter we look at the cash book, which is used to record the money transactions of the business, such as receiving payments from customers, and making payments to suppliers and for other expenses. Such money transactions are received and paid either in cash, by cheque, BACS (the bank computer payment transfer system), debit or credit card.

We see how the cash book fits into the accounting system as the book of prime entry for money transactions and as part of the double-entry system.

We look at the layout of the cash book, with money columns for bank, Value Added Tax, and settlement discount.

The cash book is usually controlled by the cashier of the business and we see a completed cash book which has been written up by the cashier. We will make transfers of data from a completed cash book to the general ledger, sales ledger and purchases ledger. Included in this data are transfers in respect of:

- cash sales
- cash purchases
- settlement discounts allowed
- settlement discounts received
- receipts from customers
- payments to suppliers
- other payments and receipts, eg general expenses, loans received and repaid

Note:
In this chapter we use the following International Accounting Standards terms:
- 'receivable' – a term which has the same meaning as 'debtor' or 'customer'
- 'payable' – a term which has the same meaning as 'creditor' or 'supplier'
- 'non-current asset' – a term which means 'fixed asset'

THE CASH BOOK IN THE ACCOUNTING SYSTEM

The cash book is used to record the money transactions of the business. It is the book of prime entry for bank receipts and payments.

In the accounting system the cash book may combine the roles of the book of prime entry and double-entry book-keeping. This means that the cash book is:
- the book of prime entry for bank receipts and payments
- the double-entry account for bank (kept in general ledger)

An alternative accounting system is where the cash book is used only as the book of prime entry. This requires a separate bank control account (see page 168) to be kept in general ledger in order to complete double-entry book-keeping.

Note that, as well as the cash book, businesses often have a petty cash book which is used for low-value cash payments for purchases and expenses. We will study petty cash book in the next chapter.

USES OF THE CASH BOOK

The cash book records the money transactions of the business, such as:

receipts
- from cash sales
- from receivables (debtors/credit customers)
- loans from the bank
- VAT refunds
- capital introduced by the owner
- transfer of money from a bank deposit account

payments
- for cash purchases
- to payables (creditor/suppliers)
- for expenses
- for bank loan repayments
- for VAT payments
- for the purchase of capital items, eg a car
- for drawings (money taken by the owner of the business for personal use)
- transfer of money to a bank deposit account

Note that the cash book is the record kept by the business of its bank transactions – the bank will keep its own records, and bank statements will either be sent regularly or will be available on-line through internet banking.

The cash book is controlled by the cashier who:

- records receipts and payments through the bank
- makes payments, and prepares cheques and bank transfers for signature by those authorised to sign
- pays cash and cheques received into the bank

It is important to note that transactions passing through the cash book must be supported by documentary evidence. As a result of this a link will be established that can be followed through the accounting system to ensure that it is complete. This link runs through:

- financial document
- book of prime entry
- double-entry accounts

This linking of the transactions is required both as a security feature within the business (to help to ensure that false and fraudulent transactions cannot be made), and also for taxation purposes.

The cashier has an important role to play within the accounting function of a business – most business activities will, at some point, involve a money transaction of either a receipt or a payment. The cash book and the cashier are therefore at the hub of the accounting system.

LAYOUT OF THE CASH BOOK

Although a cash book can be set out in many formats to suit the requirements of a particular business, a common format is the columnar cash book. This is set out in the same way as a double-entry account, with debit and credit sides, but there may be several money columns on each side. An example of a three column cash book (three money columns on each side) is shown below:

Dr						Cash Book					Cr
Date	Details	Ref	Discount allowed	VAT	Bank	Date	Details	Ref	Discount received	VAT	Bank
			£	£	£				£	£	£
			money in						money out		

Note the following points:

- The bank column on the debit side is used for money in, ie bank receipts.

- The bank column on the credit side is used for money out, ie bank payments.

- A second money column is used to record the amount of VAT, for example charged on cash sales (on the debit side) or paid on cash purchases and expenses (on the credit side). The VAT columns are not part of the double-entry system – they are used in the cash book as a listing device or memorandum column. As we will see – later in the chapter – they are totalled and transferred into the double-entry system.

- A further money column on each side is used to record settlement (cash) discount (that is, an allowance offered for quick settlement of the amount due, eg 2% cash discount for settlement within seven days).

- The discount column on the debit side is for settlement discount allowed to customers.

- The discount received column on the credit side is for settlement discount received from suppliers.

- The discount columns are not part of the double-entry system – they are used in the cash book as a listing device or memorandum column. As we will see – later in the chapter – they are totalled and transferred into the double-entry system.

- The reference column is used to code or cross-reference to the other entry in the ledger system.

Tutorial note: For *Basic Accounting 1* you are not required to make entries in the cash book; however you will have to transfer information from the cash book into the general ledger and the subsidiary sales and purchases ledgers.

Two Case Studies now follow. The first, below, uses only the bank columns of the three column cash book; the second, on page 156, includes use of the discount and VAT columns. In both Case Studies we see how the data is transferred from cash book into the double-entry book-keeping system.

Case Study 1

JAYNE HAMPSON – CASH BOOK

situation

The following cash book shows a number of transactions of a new business set up by Jayne Hampson on 30 June 20-8:

Dr						Cash Book					CB52	Cr
Date	Details	Ref	Discount allowed	VAT	Bank	Date	Details	Ref	Discount received	VAT	Bank
20-8			£	£	£	20-8			£	£	£
30 Jun	Capital	GL3100			10,000	30 Jun	Vehicle	GL0750			7,500
30 Jun	Loan from bank	GL2140			2,000	30 Jun	Rent	GL6350			500
						30 Jun	Wages	GL6380			750
						30 Jun	Drawings	GL3200			250
						30 Jun	Balance c/d				3,000
					12,000						12,000
1 Jul	Balance b/d				3,000						

Notes:

- Money in – eg capital introduced – has been recorded on the debit side, ie the business has gained value

- Money out – eg rent and wages paid – has been recorded on the credit side, ie the business has given value

- The balance of the cash book has been calculated as the difference between money in and money out, ie receipts minus payments equals the balance. Balancing of accounts is usually carried out at the end of each month where the balance is *carried down (c/d)* to the first day of the next month where it is *brought down (b/d)*. We will look in more detail at balancing accounts in Chapter 10.

solution

From the completed cash book, we need to transfer the data into the double-entry system. To do this we need to:

- identify on which side of the cash book the transaction has been recorded – debit (money in), or credit (money out)

- record the other double-entry transaction on the opposite side of the appropriate account

The other accounts from this cash book can now be recorded and, over the next few pages, we will look at each transaction and see how each is recorded in the double-entry book-keeping system.

The page of the cash book is coded CB52 and this will be the cross-reference for the other ledger accounts.

Note that in this Case Study there are no entries in the Discount or VAT columns. These columns will be illustrated and explained in the second Case Study on page 156.

CAPITAL

Capital is the amount of money invested in the business by the owner. The amount is owed by the business back to the owner, although it is unlikely to be repaid immediately as the business would cease to exist. A capital account is used to record the amount paid into the business; the book-keeping entries are:

capital introduced

- debit cash book bank column
- credit capital account

The capital transaction from Jayne Hampson's cash book is entered in capital account as follows:

GENERAL LEDGER

Dr			**Capital Account** (GL3100)		Cr
20-8		£	20-8		£
			30 Jun Bank	CB52	10,000

Note: the introduction of capital into a business is often the very first business transaction entered into the double-entry system.

LOANS

loan received

When a business receives a loan, eg from the bank, it is the bank column of cash book which is debited, while a loan account (in the name of the lender) is credited:

- debit cash book bank column
- credit loan account (in the name of the lender)

The loan transaction from Jayne Hampson's cash book is entered in loan account as follows:

GENERAL LEDGER

Dr			**Bank: Loan Account** (GL2140)		Cr
20-8		£	20-8		£
			30 Jun Bank	CB52	2,000

A loan repayment, on the other hand (not shown in the Case Study), is recorded the opposite way round to a loan received because money is being paid from the bank to repay the lender. Therefore loan account is debited and the bank column of cash book is credited (see page 165 for an example):

–   debit loan account

–   credit cash book bank column

NON-CURRENT ASSETS (FIXED ASSETS)

Non-current assets (also known as **fixed assets**) are items purchased by a business for use on a long-term basis. Examples are premises, motor vehicles, machinery and office equipment. All of these are bought by a business with the intention that they will be used for some time in the business. Without non-current assets, it would be difficult to continue in business, eg without machinery it would prove difficult to run a factory; without delivery vans and lorries it would be difficult to transport the firm's products to its customers.

When a business buys non-current assets, the expenditure is referred to as **capital expenditure**. This means that items have been bought for use in the business for some years to come. By contrast, **revenue expenditure** is where the items bought will be used by the business quite quickly. For example, the purchase of a car is capital expenditure, while the cost of fuel for the car is revenue expenditure. (Note that capital income and expenditure, and revenue income and expenditure are discussed more fully in Chapter 10.)

non-current assets and double-entry book-keeping

When non-current assets are bought, a separate account for each type of non-current asset is used in general ledger, eg premises account, motor vehicles account, machinery account, etc. The book-keeping entries are:

purchase of a non-current asset

–   debit non-current asset account (using the appropriate account)

–   credit cash book bank column

The non-current asset transaction in Jayne Hampson's cash book is entered in vehicles account as follows:

GENERAL LEDGER

Dr			**Motor Vehicles Account** (GL0750)			Cr
20-8			£	20-8		£
30 Jun	Bank	CB52	7,500			

PAYMENTS FOR EXPENSES

Businesses pay various expenses such as rent, wages, electricity, telephone, vehicle running expenses, etc. These day-to-day expenses of running the business are termed **revenue expenditure**. A separate account is used in general ledger for each main class of revenue expenditure, eg rent account, wages account, etc.

The book-keeping entries are:

payment of an expense

- debit expense account (using the appropriate account)
- credit cash book bank column

The two expenses transactions in Jayne Hampson's cash book are entered in the expenses accounts as follows:

GENERAL LEDGER

Dr			**Rent Account** (GL6350)		Cr
20-8		£	20-8		£
30 Jun	Bank	CB52	500		

Dr			**Wages Account** (GL6380)		Cr
20-8		£	20-8		£
30 Jun	Bank	CB52	750		

DRAWINGS

Drawings is the term used when the owner takes money from the business for personal use. A drawings account is used to record such amounts; the book-keeping entries for withdrawal of money are:

owner's drawings

- debit drawings account
- credit cash book bank column

The transaction in Jayne Hampson's cash book is entered in drawings account as follows:

GENERAL LEDGER

Dr				**Drawings Account** (GL3200)			Cr
20-8			£	20-8			£
30 Jun	Bank	CB52	250				

Case Study 2

FASHION TRADING – CASH BOOK

situation

This cash book develops the theme seen in the first example cash book (page 151) and includes transactions which require the use of the discount and VAT columns. The transactions are for a business called 'Fashion Trading'.

Dr						**Cash Book**				**CB28**		Cr
Date	Details	Ref	Discount allowed	VAT	Bank	Date	Details	Ref	Discount received	VAT	Bank
20-8			£	£	£	20-8			£	£	£
30 Nov	Balance b/d				1,110	30 Nov	Cash purchases	GL5100		7	47
30 Nov	Cash sales	GL4100		70	470	30 Nov	Wyvern Supplies	GL2350/			
30 Nov	Mercia Clothes	GL1200/					(payable/creditor)	PL560	25		1,100
	(receivable/debtor)	SL440	10		590	30 Nov	General expenses	GL6140		35	235
30 Nov	Commission					30 Nov	Fixtures and fittings	GL1100		210	1,410
	received	GL4390		14	94	30 Nov	Loan repayment	GL2140			750
30 Nov	Transfer from bank										
	deposit account	GL0850			1,000						
30 Nov	Balance c/d				278						
			10	84	3,542				25	252	3,542
			GL6310	GL2200					GL4360	GL2200	
						1 Dec	Balance b/d				278

Remember that money in is recorded on the debit side of cash book, ie the business has gained value; money out is recorded on the credit side, ie the business has given value.

solution

We will now look at each transaction from this cash book in the text in more detail over the next few pages and see how each is recorded in the double-entry book-keeping system.

Note that the page of the cash book is coded CB28 and this will be the cross-reference for the other ledger accounts.

BALANCES

30 Nov Balance b/d

This cash book is not for the first month of the business (contrast with Jayne Hampson's cash book for a new business on page 152), it commences with an opening balance of £1,110. This is described as 'balance b/d', ie brought down from the previous page of the cash book. (Note that this can also be written as 'balance b/f', ie brought forward from the previous page.)

As the opening balance brought down is on the debit side of the cash book this means that, according to the cash book, the business has £1,110 in the bank.

30 Nov Balance c/d

The firm's cashier has calculated the balance of cash book to be £278. This has been done by adding up the debit and credit columns of the cash book and putting the difference (ie the balance) on the smaller side – here £278 on the debit side. In this way the two money columns for bank in this example total to £3,542.

We will look in more detail at balancing accounts in Chapter 10.

1 Dec Balance b/d

To complete the double-entry book-keeping the balance of £278 is brought down on the credit side. Note that the date is the first day of the next month, ie 1 December.

As the balance brought down on 1 December is on the credit side of the cash book, this means that, according to the cash book, the business has an overdraft at the bank of £278.

CASH SALES AND CASH PURCHASES

cash sales

Cash sales are where a customer of the business buys goods or services and pays in full immediately – either in cash, by cheque, BACS, debit or credit card. The book-keeping entries are:

- debit cash book bank column with the money amount received (£470)
- debit cash book VAT column* with the amount of VAT on the sale (£70)
- credit sales account with the amount of the bank column less the amount of the VAT column £(400)

* see page 164 for transfer of the VAT column to VAT account

The cash sales transaction in Fashion Trading's cash book is entered in sales account as follows:

GENERAL LEDGER

Dr		**Sales Account** (GL4100)		Cr
20-8	£	20-8		£
		30 Nov Bank	CB28	*400

* amount of bank column less amount of VAT column

cash purchases

Cash purchases are where a business buys goods from a supplier and pays in full immediately – either in cash, by cheque, BACS, debit or credit card. The book-keeping entries are:

- debit purchases account with the amount of the bank column less the amount of the VAT column
- credit cash book bank column with the money amount paid
- credit cash book VAT column* with the amount of VAT on the purchase

* see page 164 for transfer of the VAT column to VAT account

The cash purchases transaction in Fashion Trading's cash book is entered in purchases account as follows:

GENERAL LEDGER

Dr			**Purchases Account** (GL5100)		Cr
20-8		£	20-8		£
30 Nov Bank	CB28	*40			

* amount of bank column less amount of VAT column

RECEIPTS FROM CUSTOMERS AND PAYMENTS TO SUPPLIERS

receipts from customers (receivables)

When customers pay for goods or services that have been sold to them on credit they will make payment either in cash, by cheque, BACS, debit or credit card. The book-keeping entries are:

– debit cash book bank column with the money amount received

– credit sales ledger control account (in general ledger) with the money amount received

– credit the customer's memorandum account (in sales ledger) with the money amount received

If there is settlement discount shown against the receipt in the cash book discount allowed column, another book-keeping entry is needed:

– credit the customer's memorandum account (in sales ledger) with the amount of discount allowed (see page 163 for transfer of the total of discount allowed column to discount allowed account and sales ledger control account)

Note that, for receipts from receivables (customers), no entry is shown in the cash book VAT column because VAT has been changed on invoices issued and has been recorded as a credit to VAT account (through sales day book) when the credit sale was made (see Chapter 3).

The receipt from Mercia Clothes, a customer, in Fashion Trading's cash book is entered in the ledgers as follows (the discount allowed entry to sales ledger control account is explained on page 163):

GENERAL LEDGER

Dr		Sales Ledger Control Account (GL1200)			Cr
20-8		£	20-8		£
			30 Nov Bank	CB28	590
			30 Nov Discount allowed	CB28	10

SALES LEDGER

Dr		Mercia Clothes (SL440)			Cr
20-8		£	20-8		£
			30 Nov Bank	CB28	590
			30 Nov Discount allowed	CB28	10

payments to suppliers (payables)

When businesses pay their suppliers for goods that have been bought on credit they can make payment either in cash, by cheque, BACS, debit or credit card. The book-keeping entries are:

– debit purchases ledger control account (in general ledger) with the money amount paid

– debit the supplier's memorandum account (in purchases ledger) with the money amount paid

– credit cash book bank column with the money amount paid

If there is settlement discount shown against the payment in the cash book discount received column, another book-keeping entry is needed:

– debit the supplier's memorandum account (in purchases ledger) with the amount of discount received (see page 163 for transfer of the total of discount received column to discount received account and purchases ledger control account)

Note that, for payments to payables (suppliers), no entry is shown in the cash book VAT column because VAT has been charged on invoices received and has already been recorded as a debit to VAT account (through purchases day book) when the credit purchase was made (see Chapter 6).

The payment to Wyvern Supplies, a supplier, in Fashion Trading's cash book is entered in the ledgers as follows:

GENERAL LEDGER

Dr		**Purchases Ledger Control Account** (GL2350)				Cr
20-8				£	20-8	£
30 Nov	Bank		CB28	1,100		
30 Nov	Discount received	CB28		25		

PURCHASES LEDGER

Dr		**Wyvern Supplies** (PL560)				Cr
20-8				£	20-8	£
30 Nov	Bank		CB28	1,100		
30 Nov	Discount received	CB28		25		

EXPENSES AND INCOME WITH VAT

payment of an expense, with VAT

We have seen (page 155) how payments for expenses – revenue expenditure – are recorded in the ledger system. Where a payment in cash book includes an amount of VAT, we must allow for the VAT in the book-keeping system, as follows:

– debit expense account (in general ledger) with the amount of the bank column less the amount of the VAT column

– credit cash book bank column with the money amount paid

– credit cash book VAT column with the amount of VAT on the expense (see page 164 for transfer of the VAT column to VAT account)

The expense payment in Fashion Trading's cash book is entered in general expenses account as follows:

GENERAL LEDGER

Dr			General Expenses Account (GL6140)		Cr
20-8			£	20-8	£
30 Nov	Bank	CB28	*200		

* amount of bank column less amount of VAT column

receipts for income, with VAT

Sometimes businesses have receipts for income from various sources, eg rent received, commission received. Such income is in addition to the main revenue income from the sales of the business. Where a receipt in cash book includes an amount of VAT we must allow for the VAT in the book-keeping system as follows:

– debit cash book bank column with the money amount received

– debit cash book VAT column* with the amount of VAT on the income

– credit income amount (in general ledger) with the amount of the bank column less the amount of the VAT column

* see page 164 for transfer of the VAT column to VAT account

The income receipt in Fashion Trading's cash book is entered in commission received account as follows:

GENERAL LEDGER

Dr	**Commission received** (GL4390)		Cr
20-8	£	20-8	£
		30 Nov Bank	CB28 *80

* amount of bank column less amount of VAT column

NON-CURRENT (FIXED) ASSETS WITH VAT

We have seen (on page 154) how payments for non-current assets – capital expenditure – are recorded in the ledger system. Where a payment in cash book includes an amount of VAT we must allow for the VAT in the book-keeping system as follows:

- debit non-current asset account (using the appropriate account) with the amount of the bank column, *less* the amount of the VAT column

- credit cash book bank column with the amount of money paid

- credit cash book VAT column with the amount of VAT on the non-current asset (see page 164 for transfer of the VAT column to VAT account)

The non-current asset transaction in Fashion Trading's cash book is entered in fixtures and fittings account as follows:

GENERAL LEDGER

Dr	**Fixtures and Fittings Account** (GL1100)		Cr
20-8	£	20-8	£
30 Nov Bank	CB28 *1,200		

* amount of bank column less amount of VAT column

DEALING WITH THE CASH BOOK DISCOUNT COLUMNS

In the cash book there are two columns for settlement discount. On the **debit side** is **discount allowed** by a business to its customers who settle amounts due within the period for cash discount stated on the sales invoice. On the **credit side** is **discount received** by a business from its suppliers for quick settlement within the period for cash discount stated on the supplier's invoice. These cash book columns are not part of double-entry book-keeping but they must be transferred into the book-keeping system.

Instead of recording separate amounts in the discount allowed and discount received accounts every time payments are received from customers or made to suppliers, the cash book columns are used as listing devices. There may well be several discount amounts on a page of the cash book – it is the total of the columns that is transferred into the general ledger in the book-keeping system as follows:

discount allowed

- – debit discount allowed account
- – credit sales ledger control account

discount received

- – debit purchases ledger control account
- – credit discount received account

This completes the double-entry for settlement discount. Note that amounts for discount allowed and discount received have been recorded already in the memorandum accounts of customers and suppliers in sales ledger and purchases ledger respectively.

The discount columns in Fashion Trading's cash book are entered in general ledger as follows:

GENERAL LEDGER

Dr				Discount Allowed Account (GL6310)			Cr
20-8			£	20-8			£
30 Nov	Bank	CB28	10				

Dr		Sales Ledger Control Account (GL1200)				Cr
20-8		£	20-8			£
			30 Nov Discount allowed	CB28	10	

Dr		Discount Received Account (GL4360)				Cr
20-8		£	20-8			£
			30 Nov Bank	CB28	25	

Dr				Purchases Ledger Control Account (GL2350)		Cr
20-8			£	20-8		£
30 Nov	Discount received	CB28	25			

DEALING WITH THE VAT COLUMNS

The two VAT columns of the cash book are used as listing devices, as there may well be several VAT amounts on a page of the cash book. They are not part of double-entry book-keeping in themselves, but the VAT listed by them is included in the amounts of the bank receipts and payments columns.

The totals of the VAT columns are transferred into general ledger in the book-keeping system as follows:

– debit VAT account with the total of the cash book credit side VAT column

– credit VAT account with the total of the cash book debit side VAT column

This completes double-entry book-keeping for receipts and payments which include VAT:

- the gross figure (ie including VAT) for the receipt or payment is entered in cash book

- the net figure (ie excluding VAT) is entered to the appropriate general ledger account

- VAT amounts are entered in cash book and the totals are transferred to VAT account on the opposite side to cash book

The VAT columns in Fashion Trading's cash book are transferred to VAT account as follows:

GENERAL LEDGER

Dr		**Value Added Tax Account** (GL2200)			Cr
20-8		£	20-8		£
30 Nov Bank	CB28	252	30 Nov Bank	CB28	84

OTHER CASH BOOK TRANSFERS

bank loans

loan from bank

We have already seen the double-entry book-keeping to record a loan from the bank. The book-keeping entries are:

– debit cash book bank column

– credit bank loan account

loan repayment

The book-keeping entries to repay a loan, or part of a loan, are:

- – debit bank loan account
- – credit cash book bank column

The loan repayment in Fashion Trading's cash book is entered in the bank loan account in the books of the business as follows (and will also be recorded by the bank in its own accounting records):

GENERAL LEDGER

Dr			Bank Loan Account			Cr
20-8		£	20-8			£
30 Nov	Bank	750				

transfers to and from bank deposit accounts

Many businesses have more than one bank account – eg a deposit account used for the short-term deposit of surplus funds, or a second bank current account used for specific purposes. Transfers to and from such bank accounts are recorded through cash book (and will also be recorded by the bank in its own accounting records).

transfer to bank deposit (or other) account

The book-keeping entries to make a transfer to the account are:

- – debit bank deposit (or other) account
- – credit cash book bank column

transfer from bank deposit (or other) account

The book-keeping entries to make a transfer from the account are:

- – debit cash book bank column
- – credit bank deposit (or other) account

The transfer from bank deposit account in Fashion Trading's cash book is entered in bank deposit account as follows:

GENERAL LEDGER

Dr			Bank Deposit Account (GL0850)			Cr
20-8		£	20-8			£
			30 Nov Bank	CB28	1,000	

Value Added Tax

We have seen both in earlier chapters and in this chapter how VAT-registered businesses keep a VAT account in general ledger to record the amount of VAT on sales invoices issued to customers, on invoices received from suppliers, and on running expenses and other receipts and payments. At regular intervals each business must account to HM Revenue & Customs and either pay over the money due or receive a refund. These payments or receipts of refunds are recorded through cash book.

payment of VAT to HM Revenue & Customs

The book-keeping entries are:

– debit Value Added Tax account

– credit cash book bank column

receipt of refund of VAT from HM Revenue & Customs

The book-keeping entries are:

– debit cash book bank column

– credit Value Added Tax account

HOW CASH BOOK FITS INTO THE ACCOUNTING SYSTEM

Over the past few pages we have looked at a number of bank receipts and payments which are recorded firstly in the cash book and secondly in the ledger system of general ledger, sales ledger and purchases ledger. As the cash book is the first place in the accounting system to record bank transactions, it is a **book of prime entry** for bank receipts and payments.

In most accounting systems, cash book also performs the function of being a **double-entry account** – ie a debit entry made in cash book will be recorded on the credit side of another double-entry account. The diagram on the next page shows cash book performing these two functions within the accounting system:

• as the book of prime entry for bank receipts and payments

• as an integral part of the double-entry system

The diagram shows the flow involving:

• financial documents – primary records for bank receipts and payments

• the cash book as a book of prime entry

• double-entry book-keeping, involving cash book and other ledgers

You should also note that in some accounting systems the cash book is used only as a book of prime entry with a separate bank control account in the general ledger. This alternative system is explained fully on page 168.

cash book as a book of prime entry and double-entry account

CASH BOOK RECEIPTS

- sale receipts
- sales invoices
- remittance advice notes
- debit/ credit card receipts
- paying-in slip counterfoils
- BACS receipts
- bank statements

CASH BOOK PAYMENTS

- purchase receipts
- purchases invoices
- cheque counterfoils
- debit/credit card payments
- standing orders
- direct debits
- bank charges and interest
- BACS payments
- bank statements

book of prime entry

CASH BOOK

financial documents (primary records)

debit   credit

financial documents (primary records)

double-entry book-keeping

credit

GENERAL LEDGER

- bank deposit account
- bank loan account
- capital account
- discount received account (total from discount received column on credit side of cash book)
- income received accounts
- sales account
- sales ledger control account
- VAT account

debit

GENERAL LEDGER

- bank deposit account
- bank loan account
- discount allowed account (total from discount allowed column on debit side of cash book)
- drawings account
- expenses accounts
- non-current asset accounts
- purchases account
- purchases ledger control account
- VAT account

credit

SALES LEDGER

- customers' memorandum accounts (money received, discount allowed)

debit

PURCHASES LEDGER

- suppliers' memorandum accounts (money paid, discount received)

BANK CONTROL ACCOUNT

The last two pages have explained and illustrated the common accounting system which has a cash book which fulfils the dual function of:

• a book of prime entry, and also

• the double-entry account for bank

There is a less common alternative, however, where an accounting system treats the cash book **solely as a book of prime entry**. In this situation a **bank control account** is set up in general ledger to complete the double-entry.

This account shows the total receipts and payments made through the bank during the period, together with opening and closing balances.

Suppose Fashion Trading in the Case Study (see page 156) adopted this system. In the cash book the totals of the receipts and payments from the bank columns would be entered in a bank control account (which has been given the account number GL0160) as follows:

GENERAL LEDGER

Dr			**Bank Control Account** (GL0160)			Cr
20-8		£	20-8			£
30 Nov Balance b/d		1,110	30 Nov Cash Book**	CB28		3,542
30 Nov Cash Book*	CB28	2,154				
30 Nov Balance c/d		278				
		3,542				3,542
			1 Dec Balance b/d			278

  * total of bank receipts (excluding balances b/d and c/d)

 ** total of bank payments (excluding balances b/d and c/d)

In bank control account, the cross reference to cash book enables a transaction to be followed through the accounting system – from book of prime entry to double-entry account – to ensure that it is complete.

As mentioned above, a separate bank control account is a less common arrangement. It is possible, however, that you may come across it, and so it is important to know how it functions.

Chapter Summary

■ The cash book records the money transactions of the business in the form of bank receipts and payments.

■ Receipts are recorded on the debit side; payments are recorded on the credit side.

■ A common form of cash book is the three-column cash book with columns for bank, VAT, and settlement discount.

■ Transactions recorded in the cash book include:
  – cash sales
  – cash purchases
  – settlement discount allowed
  – settlement discount received
  – receipts from customers
  – payments to suppliers
  – other payments and receipts, eg general expenses, loans received and paid

■ Cash book may combine the roles of:
  – the book of prime entry for bank receipts and payments
  – the double-entry account for bank

■ When the cash book is used only as the book of prime entry, a bank control account is used in general ledger to complete double-entry book-keeping.

■ The total of the discount allowed column in cash book is transferred to the double-entry system as:
  – debit discount allowed account
  – credit sales ledger control account

■ The total of the discount received column in cash book is transferred to the double-entry system as:
  – debit purchases ledger control account
  – credit discount received account

■ The total of the VAT columns in cash book are transferred to the double-entry system as:
  – debit VAT account, with the total of the cash book credit side VAT column
  – credit VAT account, with the total of the cash book debit side VAT column

Key Terms		
	cash book	records bank receipts and payments; may combine the roles of the book of prime entry for bank receipts and payments and the double-entry account for bank
	three-column cash book	cash book with columns for bank, VAT, and settlement discount
	capital	the amount of money invested in the business by the owner
	capital expenditure	the purchase of non-current assets for use in the business
	revenue expenditure	day-to-day expenses of running a business
	drawings	when the owner takes money from the business for personal use
	cash sales	where a customer buys goods or services and pays in full immediately
	cash purchases	where a business buys goods from a supplier and pays in full immediately
	discount allowed	amount allowed by a business to its customers who settle amounts due within the period for cash discount stated on the sales invoice
	discount received	amount received by a business from its suppliers for quick settlement within the period for cash discount stated on the supplier's invoice
	bank control account	double-entry account in general ledger used when cash book is treated solely as the book of prime entry; it shows the total receipts and payments made by the cashier during the period, together with the opening and closing balances

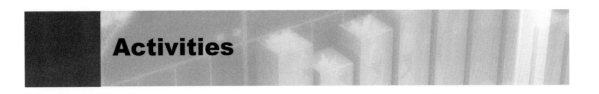

Activities

8.1 The cash book is often:

(a) a financial document

(b) the account kept by the bank of its customer's bank receipts and payments

(c) a part of double-entry book-keeping only

(d) the book of prime entry and double-entry account for bank receipts and payments

Answer (a) or (b) or (c) or (d)

8.2 A business has made a cash sale for £800 plus VAT at 17.5% to a customer who does not have a credit account. Which one of the following is correct double-entry book-keeping to record the sale?

(a) debit bank £800, debit VAT £140, credit sales £940

(b) debit bank £940, credit sales £800, credit VAT £140

(c) debit bank £800, debit VAT £140, credit sales £940

(d) debit sales £800, debit VAT £140, credit bank £940

Answer (a) or (b) or (c) or (d)

8.3 The following cash book shows a number of transactions of a new business set up by Hannah Wyrembak on 30 April 20-7:

Dr							Cash Book				CB70	Cr
Date	Details	Ref	Discount allowed	VAT	Bank	Date	Details	Ref	Discount received	VAT	Bank
			£	£	£				£	£	£
20-7						20-7					
30 Apr	Capital				8,000	30 Apr	Rent				1,000
30 Apr	Loan from bank				5,000	30 Apr	Wages				800
						30 Apr	Drawings				500
						30 Apr	Vehicle				10,000
						30 Apr	Balance c/d				700
					13,000						13,000
1 May	Balance b/d				700						

You are to transfer the data from the cash book into the double-entry system of Hannah Wyrembak. Note that a bank control account is not required.

8.4   The following transactions all took place on 31 May 20-6 and have been entered into the cash book of John Singer, as shown below. No entries have yet been made into the ledger system.

Dr				**Cash Book**			**CB64**	Cr
Date	Details	VAT	Bank	Date	Details		VAT	Bank
20-6		£	£	20-6			£	£
31 May	Balance b/d		3,840	31 May	Wages			1,175
31 May	T Jones (receivable)		2,750	31 May	Rent			1,200
31 May	Cash sales	70	470	31 May	Drawings			600
				31 May	Bank loan repayment			750
				31 May	Balance c/d			3,335
		70	7,060					7,060
1 Jun	Balance b/d		3,335					

Note that John Singer's accounting system does not use a bank control account.

(a)   What will be the entries in the sales ledger of John Singer?

Sales ledger

Account name	Amount £	Debit ✓	Credit ✓

(b)   What will be the entries in the general ledger of John Singer?

General ledger

Account name	Amount £	Debit ✓	Credit ✓

8.5   The following cash book shows a number of transactions of Teme Traders which all took place on 30 April 20-5:

Dr											Cr
				Cash Book						**CB32**	
Date	Details	Ref	Discount allowed	VAT	Bank	Date	Details	Ref	Discount received	VAT	Bank
20-5			£	£	£	20-5			£	£	£
30 Apr	Balance b/d				2,080	30 Apr	Mereford Mills				
30 Apr	Cash sales			35	235		(payable)		50		3,200
30 Apr	Commission					30 Apr	Cash purchases			14	94
	received			7	47	30 Apr	Office equipment			350	2,350
30 Apr	Lindum Ltd					30 Apr	Wages				1,550
	(receivable)		40		2,400	30 Apr	General expenses			70	470
30 Apr	Loan from bank				2,000						
30 Apr	Balance c/d				902						
			40	42	7,664				50	434	7,664
						1 May	Balance b/d				902

(a)   The balance brought down of £2,080 on 30 April shows that, according to the cash book, the business has money in the bank. True or false?

(b)   The balance brought down of £902 on 1 May shows that, according to the cash book, the business has money in the bank. True or false?

(c)   You are to transfer the data from the cash book into the double-entry system of Teme Traders. Note that a bank control account is not required.

8.6   At the end of the month, the cash book of a business has a total of £80 for discount received and a total of £120 for discount allowed. Which one of the following is correct double-entry to record the settlement discount?

(a)   debit discount allowed £120, credit discount received £80

(b)   debit discount allowed £40

(c)   debit discount received £80, credit discount allowed £120

(d)   debit discount received £40

Answer (a) or (b) or (c) or (d)

9 Petty cash book

this chapter covers...

In this chapter we look at the petty cash book, which is used to record low-value cash payments for small purchases and expenses incurred by a business. Examples of these payments include the purchase of office stationery items, and the payment of travel expenses.

We see how the petty cash book fits into the accounting system as a book of prime entry for low-value cash payments and as part of the double-entry system.

We describe the layout of the petty cash book, with analysis columns for expenses.

The petty cash book is usually controlled by a member of staff who is given the responsibility of being the petty cashier of the business.

In the chapter we will describe a completed petty cash book which has been written up by the petty cashier. We will make transfers of data from a completed petty cash book to the general ledger accounts.

THE PETTY CASH BOOK IN THE ACCOUNTING SYSTEM

The petty cash book is used to record low-value cash payments for purchases and expenses – such as small items of stationery, postages, etc. Items like these are not appropriate to enter in the cash book because they would 'clutter' it up with lots of small amounts. Instead a member of staff is given the responsibility of being the firm's petty cashier. Petty cash book is the book of prime entry for low-value cash payments.

In the accounting system the petty cash book may combine the roles of the book of prime entry and double-entry book-keeping. This means that the petty cash book is:

- the book of prime entry for low-value cash payments
- the double-entry account for petty cash (kept in general ledger)

An alternative accounting system is where the petty cash book is kept as the book of prime entry only. This means that a separate petty cash control account (see page 184) is kept in general ledger in order to complete the double-entry book-keeping.

USES OF THE PETTY CASH BOOK

The petty cash book records the low-value cash payments for purchases and expenses of the business, such as:

- stationery items
- small items of office supplies
- casual wages
- window cleaning
- bus, rail and taxi fares incurred on behalf of the business
- meals and drinks incurred on behalf of the business
- postages
- tips and donations

Petty cash payments are usually for amounts up to a maximum value, for example, up to £25 for any one expense item.

As well as payments there may, from time-to-time, be small receipts of cash to be recorded. For example, if a member of staff purchases items such as postage stamps or stationery, they will pay the petty cashier who issues a receipt to record the details and the amount of money received.

The petty cash book is the responsibility of the petty cashier who:

- receives an amount of money (known as the petty cash float) from the firm's cashier to be used for petty cash payments

- is responsible for security of the petty cash money
- makes cash payments against authorised petty cash vouchers
- records the payments made, and analyses them in a petty cash book
- receives and records any small amounts of income, eg postage stamps sold to staff for their private use
- balances the petty cash book at regular intervals, usually weekly or monthly
- tops up the petty cash float by claiming reimbursement from the cashier of amounts paid out
- passes the completed petty cash book to the book-keeper so that data can be transferred into the ledger system

THE IMPREST SYSTEM

Petty cash books usually operate using the imprest system. With this system, the petty cashier starts each week (or month) with a certain amount of money – the imprest amount. As payments are made during the week (or month) the amount of money will reduce and, at the end of the period, the cash will be made up by a payment from bank account to restore the imprest amount. For example:

Started week with imprest amount	£100.00
Total of petty cash amounts paid out during week	£80.00
Cash held at end of week	£20.00
Amount drawn from bank to restore imprest amount	£80.00
Cash at start of next week, ie imprest amount	£100.00

If, at any time, the imprest amount proves to be insufficient, further amounts of cash can be drawn from the cashier. Also, from time-to-time, it may be necessary to increase the imprest amount so that regular shortfalls of petty cash are avoided.

PETTY CASH VOUCHERS

Petty cash vouchers are the financial documents against which payments are made out of petty cash. They are the financial documents used by the petty cashier to write up the petty cash book.

Petty cash vouchers are completed as follows:

- with the date, details and amount of expenditure
- with the signature of the person making the claim and receiving the money

- with the signature of the person authorising the payment to be made – usually the manager of the person making the claim
- additionally, most petty cash vouchers are numbered, so that they can be controlled, the number being entered in the petty cash book
- with the relevant documentation, such as a receipt from a shop or post office etc, attached to the petty cash voucher

An example petty cash voucher is as follows:

petty cash voucher		Number *47*	
		date *5 April 20-4*	
description		amount	
		£	p
Photocopier paper		*3*	*20*
VAT at 17.5%		*0*	*56*
Total		*3*	*76*
signature *T Harris*			
authorised *R Singh*			

LAYOUT OF THE PETTY CASH BOOK

Petty cash book is usually set out as follows:

Receipts	Date	Details	Voucher number	Total payment	Analysis columns				
					VAT	Postages	Stationery	Travel	Ledger
£				£	£	£	£	£	£
money in: debit side				money out: credit side					

The layout shows that:

- there are columns showing the date and details of all receipts and payments
- receipts are shown in the debit column on the extreme left
- there is a column for the petty cash voucher number
- the total payment (ie the amount paid out on each petty cash voucher) is in the next column, which is the credit side of the petty cash book
- then follow the analysis columns which analyse each transaction entered in the 'total payment' column

A business will use whatever analysis columns are most suitable for it and, indeed, there may be more columns than shown in the example.

Tutorial note: For Basic Accounting 1 you are not required to make entries in the petty cash book; however you will have to transfer data from the cash book into the general ledger (and sometimes into the subsidiary purchases ledger).

The Case Study which follows shows a petty cash book which has been written up by the petty cashier and we see how data is transferred from petty cash book into the double-entry system.

Case Study

1.850

PETTY CASH BOOK

situation

The following petty cash book has been written up by the petty cashier of Wyvern Traders for the week ended 9 April 20-4:

Petty Cash Book									PCB30
Receipts	Date	Details	Voucher number	Total payment	Analysis columns				
					VAT	Postages	Stationery	Travel	Ledger
£	20-4			£	£	£	£	£	£
100.00	5 Apr	Balance b/d							
	5 Apr	Stationery	47	3.76	0.56		3.20		
	5 Apr	Taxi fare	48	5.64	0.84			4.80	
10.00	6 Apr	Fred Dexter (postage stamps)	122						
	6 Apr	Postages	49	2.75		2.75			
	7 Apr	Taxi fare	50	9.40	1.40			8.00	
	7 Apr	J Jones (PL054)	51	15.00					15.00
	8 Apr	Stationery	52	7.05	1.05		6.00		
	8 Apr	Postages	53	5.85		5.85			
	9 Apr	Taxi fare	54	11.75	1.75			10.00	
				61.20	5.60	8.60	9.20	22.80	15.00
					GL2200	GL6330	GL6360	GL6370	GL2350
51.20	9 Apr	Bank (CB55)							
	9 Apr	Balance c/d		100.00					
161.20				161.20					
100.00	10 Apr	Balance b/d							

Notes:

- This petty cash book has been written up for the week. It is for a business to decide how often petty cash book is to be totalled and balanced – generally, though, this will be done either weekly or monthly.

- This cash book starts each new week with a cash float of £100 – this is the imprest amount. The amount of the float at the start is for the business to decide based on the level of expenses regularly paid out in petty cash – £100 may be sufficient, but larger floats may be needed. In any case, if the petty cashier runs out of cash during the week or month, a top-up can be made from cash book.

- The analysis columns are for a business to decide what is suitable for their circumstances. The ledger column is used for payments from petty cash to creditors who have accounts in purchases ledger – these suppliers are more usually paid through the bank but, if the amount is small, they may be paid in cash from petty cash.

solution

We will now see in the main text below how the data is transferred into the double-entry book-keeping system.

Note that the page of the petty cash book is coded PCB30 and this will be the cross-reference for the other ledger accounts.

BALANCES

5 Apr Balance b/d

The week commences with a petty cash book float of £100, described as 'balance b/d', ie brought down from the previous page of the petty cash book. (Note that this can also be written as 'balance b/f', ie brought forward from the previous page.) The imprest amount for this petty cash book is £100.

9 Apr Balance c/d

The firm's petty cashier has claimed reimbursement from the cashier of £51.20, ie petty cash paid out £61.20 less £10 received from Fred Dexter for postage stamps. This restores the cash float to £100 which is now recorded as the balance c/d on the credit (payments) side. The receipts and payments columns are then both totalled to £161.20.

10 Apr Balance b/d

To complete double-entry book-keeping the balance of £100 is brought down on the debit side. Note that, here, the date used in the day following the balance carried down – this shows that the cash float of £100 is ready for the next week's transactions.

TRANSFERRING THE ANALYSIS COLUMNS

In order to complete double-entry the totals of the analysis columns are transferred into the double-entry book-keeping system. The book-keeping entries are:

- payment of an expense
  - debit expense account (using the appropriate account)
- payment to a supplier (from the 'ledger' column)
  - debit purchases ledger control account (in general ledger)
  - debit the supplier's memorandum account (in purchases leger)

From the Case Study the general ledger accounts will be written up as follows at the end of the week (9 April):

GENERAL LEDGER

Dr	**Value Added Tax Account** (GL2200)		Cr
20-4		£	20-4	£
9 Apr	Petty cash book PCB30	5.60	

Dr	**Postages Account** (GL6330)		Cr
20-4		£	20-4	£
9 Apr	Petty cash book PCB30	8.60	6 Apr Petty cash book PCB30 *10.00

* cash received by the petty cashier from Fred Dexter for postage stamps purchased

Dr	**Stationery Account** (GL6360)		Cr
20-4		£	20-4	£
9 Apr	Petty cash book PCB30	9.20	

Dr	**Travel Expenses Account** (GL6370)		Cr
20-4		£	20-4	£
9 Apr	Petty cash book PCB30	22.80	

Dr	**Purchases Ledger Control Account** (GL2350)			Cr
20-4		£	20-4	£
9 Apr	Petty cash book PCB30	15.00		

The above £15 payment ledger transaction will also be debited to the account of the supplier – here J Jones – in the purchases ledger, as follows:

PURCHASES LEDGER

Dr	**J Jones** (PL054)			Cr
20-4		£	20-4	£
9 Apr	Petty cash book PCB30	15.00		

RESTORING THE CASH FLOAT

To restore the petty cash float to the imprest amount, the petty cashier completes a cheque requisition form for a cheque made payable to cash. The petty cashier takes the cheque to the bank and obtains the cash. An example of a cheque requisition is shown below:

CHEQUE REQUISITION	
Amount	*£51.20*
Payee	*Cash*
Date	*9 April 20-4*
Details	*Reimbursement of petty cash*
Signature	*Jane Watkins, petty cashier*
Authorised by	*Natalie Wilson, supervisor*
Cheque no	*017234*

cheque requisition form

The double-entry book-keeping entries to record this reimbursement are:

– *debit* petty cash book

– *credit* cash book, ie the payments side

The amount of £51.20 cash paid from the bank to the petty cashier is recorded in the cash book as follows:

Dr							Cash Book			CB55			Cr
Date	Details	Ref	Discount allowed	VAT	Bank	Date	Details	Ref	Discount received	VAT	Bank
20-4			£	£	£	20-4 9 Apr	Petty cash	PCB30	£	£	£ 51.20

After this reimbursement, the petty cash float is restored and the petty cash book has a balance brought down of £100.00 on 9 April. The petty cash book is now ready for next week's transactions.

HOW PETTY CASH BOOK FITS INTO THE ACCOUNTING SYSTEM

Over the last few pages we have seen how low-value cash payments for small purchases and expenses are recorded firstly in the petty cash book and secondly in the general ledger (and sometimes also in purchases ledger). As the petty cash book is the first place in the accounting system to record these transactions, it is a book of prime entry for low-value cash payments.

In most accounting systems, petty cash book also performs the function of being a double-entry account – ie a credit entry in petty cash book for a low-value payment will be recorded on the debit side of the account in general ledger for the small purchase or expense.

The diagram on the next page shows petty cash book performing two functions within the accounting system:

• as the **book of prime entry** for low-value cash payments

• as **part of the double-entry** system

This diagram shows the flow involving:

- financial documents – petty cash vouchers
- the petty cash book as a book of prime entry
- double-entry book-keeping, involving petty cash and the other ledgers

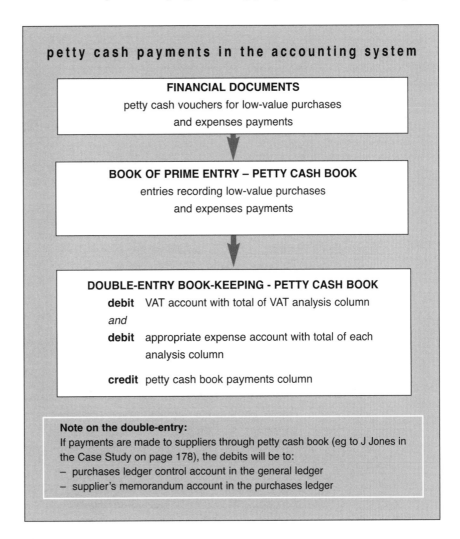

petty cash book solely as a book of prime entry

As a contrast to the above, some accounting systems treat petty cash book solely as a book of prime entry, in which case a separate double-entry account – called **petty cash control account** – is used in the general ledger. This system is less common than the system described on the last two pages.

An example of petty cash control account, using the petty cash book of Wyvern Traders (from the Case Study), is shown on the next page.

PETTY CASH CONTROL ACCOUNT

As noted above, where an accounting system treats petty cash book solely as a book of prime entry, a **petty cash control account** is used in general ledger to complete double-entry. From Wyvern Traders' petty cash book (on page 178) the totals of receipts and payments are entered in petty cash control account (which has been given the account number GL0180) as follows:

GENERAL LEDGER

Dr		£				Cr
				Petty Cash Control Account (GL0180)		
20-4		£	20-4			£
5 Apr	Balance b/d	100.00	9 Apr	Petty cash book PCB30		61.20
9 Apr	Petty cash book		9 Apr	Balance c/d		100.00
	PCB30	10.00				
9 Apr	Bank CB55	51.20				
		161.20				161.20
10 Apr	Balance b/d	100.00				

Notes:

- The debit 'balance b/d' on 5 April of £100.00 is the same as the opening balance in petty cash book – see page 178. This is the imprest amount for this petty cash book.

- The credit entry for 'petty cash book PCB30' on 9 April of £61.20 is the total of the analysis columns (VAT and expenses) from petty cash book. These amounts are debited to their respective accounts in general ledger, as already seen on pages 182 and 183.

- The debit entry for 'petty cash book PCB30' on 9 April for £10.00 is the receipt of cash from Fred Dexter – payment for the purchase of postage stamps. This amount is credited to the relevant account – here postages account – in general ledger, as already seen on page 180.

- The debit entry for 'bank CB55' on 9 April for £51.20 is the reimbursement of petty cash in order to restore the imprest amount. The cheque requisition for this is shown on page 181.

- The 'balance c/d' on 9 April (and brought down on 10 April) for £100.00 is the new balance on petty cash book, ready for next week's transactions.

- In petty cash control account, the cross reference to petty cash book enables a transaction to be followed through the accounting system – from book of prime entry to double-entry account – to ensure that it is complete.

Chapter Summary

- The petty cash book records low-value cash payments for small purchases and expenses incurred by a business.

- Petty cash receipts are recorded on the debit side; payments are recorded on the credit side.

- Transactions recorded in petty cash book include:
  - stationery items
  - small items of office supplies
  - casual wages
  - window cleaning
  - bus, rail and taxi fares incurred on behalf of the business
  - meals and drinks incurred on behalf of the business
  - postages
  - tips and donations

- Petty cash book is controlled by the petty cashier.

- The petty cashier writes up the petty cash book from petty cash vouchers, which are analysed under various expense headings.

- At regular intervals – weekly or monthly – the data from the completed petty cash book is transferred to general ledger where the total of each analysis column is debited to the relevant account.

- Petty cash book may combine the roles of:
  - the book of prime entry for low-value cash payments
  - the double-entry account for petty cash

- When the petty cash book is used only as the book of prime entry, a petty cash control account is used in general ledger to complete double-entry book-keeping.

petty cash book	records low-value cash payments for small purchases and expenses; may combine the roles of the book of prime entry for low-value cash payments and the double-entry account for petty cash
petty cashier	the person responsible for the petty cash book
petty cash voucher	financial document against which payments are made out of petty cash
imprest method	where the money held in the petty cash float is restored to the same amount for the beginning of each week or month
petty cash float	amount of money received by the petty cashier from the firm's cashier at the beginning of the period to be used for petty cash payments
analysis columns	used in petty cash book to record expense payments under various headings to suit the circumstances of the business
petty cash control account	double-entry account in general ledger used when petty cash book is treated solely as the book of prime entry; it shows the total payments made by the petty cashier during the week or month, and records receipts from bank account, together with the opening and closing balances

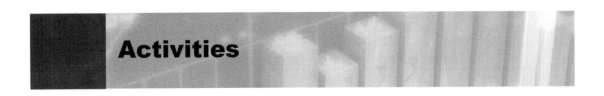

Activities

9.1 The petty cash book:

    (a)   is a financial document

    (b)   is a part of double-entry book-keeping only

    (c)   is the book of prime entry for low-value cash payments

    (d)   records and analyses expenses payments on the debit side

    Answer (a) or (b) or (c) or (d)

9.2 A petty cash voucher:

    (a)   is a financial document against which payments are made out of petty cash

    (b)   is used to draw cash from bank to top-up the petty cash float

    (c)   is passed to the book-keeper for posting to the general ledger expenses accounts

    (d)   is used to restore the imprest amount of the cash float

    Answer (a) or (b) or (c) or (d)

9.3 When the total of a petty cash book's analysis column for VAT is transferred to the VAT account in general ledger, will it be recorded as a debit or credit entry in general ledger?

	✓
Debit	
Credit	

9.4 The petty cashier of the business where you work tops up the petty cash at the end of the month with £75 withdrawn from the bank.

What will be the entries in the general ledger?

General ledger

Account name	Amount £	Debit ✓	Credit ✓

9.5 The following petty cash transactions took place in August 20-4 and have been entered into the petty cash book of Mercian Hire Company, as shown below. No entries have yet been made into the general ledger.

Receipts	Date	Details	Voucher number	Total payment	VAT	Postages	Travel	Meals	Office sundries
									Petty Cash Book
									PCB 10
						Analysis columns			
£	20-4			£	£	£	£	£	£
75.00	1 Aug	Balance b/d							
	4 Aug	Postages	223	7.20		7.20			
	6 Aug	Travel expenses	224	4.50			4.50		
	9 Aug	Postages	225	2.54		2.54			
	12 Aug	Envelopes	226	4.70	0.70				4.00
	13 Aug	Window cleaning	227	7.05	1.05				6.00
	17 Aug	Taxi fare	228	7.52	1.12		6.40		
	20 Aug	Postages	229	8.56		8.56			
	23 Aug	Meals	230	6.35				6.35	
	27 Aug	Envelopes	231	6.58	0.98				5.60
				55.00	3.85	18.30	10.90	6.35	15.60
55.00	31 Aug	Bank							
	31 Aug	Balance c/d		75.00					
130.00				130.00					
75.00	1 Sep	Balance b/d							

Note that Mercian Hire Company's accounting system does not use a petty cash control account.

Using the form below, show the entries in the general ledger (including cash book) of Mercian Hire Company.

General ledger

Account name	Amount £	Debit ✓	Credit ✓

9.6 The following petty cash book shows a number of transactions of Nelson and Company for March 20-9. The petty cash book is kept solely as a book of prime entry.

					Petty Cash Book						PCB20
Receipts	Date	Details	Voucher	Total	Analysis columns						
			number	payment	VAT	Travel	Postages	Stationery	Meals	Ledger
£	20-9			£	£	£	£	£	£	£
100.00	1 Mar	Balance b/d								
	4 Mar	Taxi fare	39	6.58	0.98	5.60				
	6 Mar	Postages	40	6.80			6.80			
	9 Mar	Pens	41	4.70	0.70			4.00		
	11 Mar	Travel expenses	42	5.46		5.46				
8.50	12 Mar	J Humphries	317							
		(postage stamps)								
	16 Mar	Envelopes	43	2.82	0.42			2.40		
	18 Mar	P Andrews (PL)	44	13.50						13.50
	19 Mar	Rail fare/meal allow	45	10.60		5.60			5.00	
	20 Mar	Postage	46	4.75			4.75			
	23 Mar	Tape	47	3.76	0.56			3.20		
	25 Mar	Postage	48	5.10			5.10			
	27 Mar	Taxi fare	49	8.93	1.33	7.60				
				73.00	3.99	24.26	16.65	9.60	5.00	13.50
64.50	31 Mar	Bank								
	31 Mar	Balance c/d		100.00						
173.00				173.00						
100.00	1 Apr	Balance b/d								

(a)   You are to transfer the data from the petty cash book into the general ledger accounts (including cash book) as at 31 March 20-9. Note that a petty cash control is required.

(b)   Show the entry that will be recorded in purchases ledger as at 31 March 20-9.

10 Balancing accounts, accounting equation, capital and revenue

this chapter covers...

In previous chapters we have seen how to record sales, purchases, expenses and other transactions in the accounts contained in general ledger, sales ledger and purchases ledger.

With the 'traditional' form of account – the 'T' account – that we have used, it is necessary to calculate the balance at regular intervals.

The balance of an account is the running total of the account to date and will tell us information such as:

- the amount of sales made
- the total amount of receivables (debtors)
- how much a particular receivable owes us
- the amount of a particular expense, such as wages
- the amount of money in the bank
- the amount of VAT due to or from HM Revenue and Customs

We will describe how the balancing of accounts is carried out.

We will then explain the accounting equation, which is another way of understanding double-entry book-keeping.

In the accounting equation we will see how the dual aspect of the debit and credit entries for each transaction are related to what happens in the equation.

Later in the chapter we look at the differences between

- capital expenditure and revenue expenditure
- capital income and revenue income

We appreciate why it is important to classify this income and expenditure correctly in the double-entry system – if this is not done, the accounts may show a false financial position for the business.

BALANCING ACCOUNTS

At regular intervals, often at the end of each month, the 'traditional' form of account – the 'T' account – needs to be balanced in order to show the running total of the account to date, for example:

- the amount of sales made (sales account)
- the total amount of receivables (debtors) – sales ledger control account
- the amount owing by a particular receivable (the customer's account in sales ledger)
- the amount of purchases made (purchases account)
- the total amount of payables (creditors) – purchases ledger control account
- the amount owing to a particular supplier (the supplier's account in purchases ledger)
- the amount of a particular expense (account for the particular expense)
- the amount of money in the bank (cash book or bank control account)
- the amount of VAT due to or from HMRC (VAT account)

When accounts are produced using a computer accounting system, there is no need to balance each account – the balance is calculated automatically after each transaction and shown in a third money column (after debit and credit) – just like a bank statement.

METHOD OF BALANCING ACCOUNTS

Accounts contained in general ledger, sales ledger and purchases ledger are balanced at regular intervals. The example set out below is a customer's account from sales ledger which has been balanced at the month-end:

Dr				Keene and Company		Cr		
20-4		❶	£	20-4			❶	£
1 Jun	Balance b/d		110	14 Jun	Bank			190
8 Jun	Sales		460	21 Jun	Sales Returns			130
17 Jun	Sales		240	30 Jun	Balance c/d		❷	630
29 Jun	Sales		140					
		❸	950				❸	950
1 Jul	Balance b/d	❹	630					

The steps involved in balancing accounts are indicated by the numbers in the boxes in the account shown on the previous page, and are described below.

Step 1

The entries in the debit and credit money columns are totalled; these totals are not recorded in ink on the account at this stage, but can be recorded either as sub-totals in pencil on the account, or noted on a separate piece of paper – nothing is entered in the account at this stage. In the example above, the debit side totals £950, while the credit side is £320.

Step 2

The difference between the two totals is the balance of the account and this is entered on the account:

- on the side of the smaller total
- on the next available line
- with the date of balancing (often the last day of the month)
- with the description 'balance c/d', or 'balance carried down'

In the account of Keene and Company above, the balance carried down is £950 – £320 = £630, entered in the credit column.

Step 3

Both sides of the account are now totalled, including the balance which has just been entered, and the totals (the same on both sides) are entered on the same line in the appropriate column, and bold-underlined or double-underlined. The underline indicates that the account has been balanced at this point using the figures above the total: the figures above the underline should not be added in to anything below the underline.

In the customer's account on the previous page the totals on each side of the account are £950.

Step 4

As we are using double-entry book-keeping, there must be an opposite entry to the 'balance c/d' calculated in Step 2. The same money amount is entered on the other side of the account below the underlined totals entered in Step 3. We have now completed both the debit and credit entry. The date is usually recorded as the next day after 'balance c/d', ie often the first day of the following month, and the description can be 'balance b/d' or 'balance brought down'.

Balance b/d

In the example on the previous page, the balance brought down on the account of 1 July 20-4 is £630 debit; this means that, according to the accounting records, Keene and Company owes £630, ie is a receivable (debtor) of the business. (You will note that the first item on the debit side of the account is '1 Jun Balance b/d £110': this shows that the account was balanced in May, with the balance brought down to June.)

a practical point:

When balancing accounts, use a pen and not a pencil (except for Step 1). If any errors are made, cross them through neatly with a single line, and write the corrected version on the line below. Do not use correcting fluid: at best it conceals errors, at worst it conceals fraudulent transactions.

FURTHER EXAMPLES OF BALANCING ACCOUNTS

Dr		**Purchases Account**			Cr
20-4		£	20-4		£
1 Apr	Balance b/d	500	30 Apr	Balance c/d	1,100
9 Apr	N Patel	250			
16 Apr	T Smith	200			
23 Apr	Lloyd & Co	150			
		1,100			1,100
1 May	Balance b/d	1,100			

The above general ledger account has transactions on one side only, but is still balanced in the same way. This account shows that, according to the accounting records, purchases to date total £1,100.

Dr		**B Lewis Limited**			Cr
20-4		£	20-4		£
1 Aug	Balance b/d	350	9 Aug	Sales Returns	350
12 Aug	Sales	150	20 Aug	Sales Returns	150
		500			500

This customer account in sales ledger has a 'nil' balance after the transactions for August have taken place. The two sides of the account are totalled and, as both debit and credit side are the same amount, there is nothing further to do, apart from entering the bold-underlined or double-underlined total.

Dr		**Sales Returns Account**			Cr
20-4		£	20-4		£
31 Jan	Sales Returns Day Book	680			

This general ledger account has just the one transaction and, in practice, there is no need to balance it. It should be clear that the account has a debit balance of £680, which is probably the sales returns for the first month of the new financial year.

Dr		**Malvern Manufacturing Company**			Cr
20-4		£	20-4		£
4 Nov	Purchases Returns	250	1 Nov	Balance b/d	250

This supplier's account in purchases ledger has a 'nil' balance, with just one transaction on each side. All that is needed here is to bold-underline or double-underline the amount on both sides.

HOW DO WE USE THE BALANCES OF ACCOUNTS?

Once accounts have been balanced, the balances of the general ledger accounts are used in the **initial trial balance** (see Chapter 11). This is a summary in two columns of the balances of all the general ledger accounts (including cash and petty cash), listing debit balances in one money column and credit balances in another. The total of each money column is shown and, if the double-entry book-keeping has been accurate in the day-to-day recording of transactions, the total of the two columns will be the same. The initial trial balance is described in more detail in the next chapter.

The balances of sales ledger accounts show how much is owed by each individual receivable (debtor). The business can send out statements of account (see page 25) to customers and the balances show how much is owed by each customer.

The balances of purchases ledger accounts show how much the business owes to each individual payable (creditor). The balances can be reconciled to the statements of account received from suppliers and will help in the preparation of payments to suppliers (see Chapter 7).

THE ACCOUNTING EQUATION

Another way of understanding double-entry book-keeping is to look at the **accounting equation**.

In Chapter 3 we saw how the principle of double-entry book-keeping is that two entries – one on the debit side and one on the credit side – are made for each financial transaction. A debit entry is made in the account which gains value, or records an asset, or an expense; a credit entry is made in the account which gives value, or records a liability, or an income item. This dual aspect is illustrated by the following diagram (which has been seen before in Chapter 3):

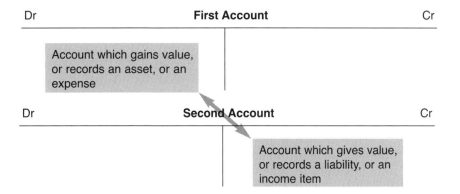

The accounting equation relates to the principles of double-entry book-keeping and states that:

assets minus **liabilities** equals **capital**

To define these terms:

- **assets** – items owned by the business, eg fixed assets, inventory (stock), bank balances, and money owed to the business by receivables (debtors)
- **liabilities** – amounts owed by the business, such as bank loans and overdrafts, and money owed by the business to payables (creditors)
- **capital** – money invested in the business by the owner

The accounting equation is illustrated in the following diagram:

assets	minus	**liabilities**	equals	**capital**
what a business owns		*what a business owes*		*the owner's investment in the business*

We will now see how the equation is affected by financial transactions made by a business.

workings of the accounting equation

Financial transactions will have an effect on the accounting equation because they result in two entries being made on opposite sides in the double-entry system. The accounting equation therefore always balances; for example, if the owner of a business starts up the business with capital of £10,000 in the business bank account, the book-keeping will show the asset of bank account (cash book) and the owner's capital account, ie

assets	minus	**liabilities**	equals	**capital**
£10,000 –		**£0**	**=**	**£10,000**
bank account				**capital account**
what a business owns		*what a business owes*		*the owner's investment in the business*

Study the following financial transactions made through the business bank account and see how the accounting equation is affected by each of the transactions.

TRANSACTION	EFFECT ON EQUATION
Business pays a supplier	• decrease in asset (bank) • decrease in liability (money owed to supplier)
Comment: assets and liabilities both decrease by the amount of the payment; capital remains unchanged.	
Business buys a computer	• increase in asset (computer) • decrease in asset (bank)
Comment: assets remain the same because the two transactions cancel each other out in the assets section: value is transferred from the asset of bank to the asset of computer.	
The owner introduces new capital by paying a cheque into the bank	• increase in asset (bank) • increase in capital (the owner's investment in the business)
Comment: both sides of the equation increase by the amount of the capital introduced.	

double-entry and the accounting equation

The diagram below shows a number of financial transactions made through the business bank account. Note in each case:

* how each financial transaction involves double-entry
* what the effects of the transaction are
* how the accounting equation changes as a result
* the fact that the accounting equation always balances after the changes

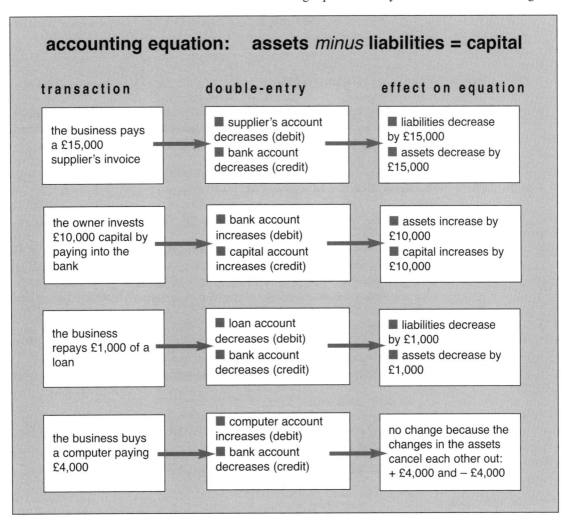

accounting equation: assets *minus* liabilities = capital

transaction	double-entry	effect on equation
the business pays a £15,000 supplier's invoice	■ supplier's account decreases (debit) ■ bank account decreases (credit)	■ liabilities decrease by £15,000 ■ assets decrease by £15,000
the owner invests £10,000 capital by paying into the bank	■ bank account increases (debit) ■ capital account increases (credit)	■ assets increase by £10,000 ■ capital increases by £10,000
the business repays £1,000 of a loan	■ loan account decreases (debit) ■ bank account decreases (credit)	■ liabilities decrease by £1,000 ■ assets decrease by £1,000
the business buys a computer paying £4,000	■ computer account increases (debit) ■ bank account decreases (credit)	no change because the changes in the assets cancel each other out: + £4,000 and − £4,000

As you can see from the double-entry transactions, the equation always balances. Each transaction has a dual aspect, with two entries involved: this is the basis of the theory of double-entry book-keeping which we have studied in this book.

CAPITAL AND REVENUE EXPENDITURE AND INCOME

In the double-entry book-keeping system, it is important to distinguish between:

- **capital expenditure** and **revenue expenditure**
- **capital income** and **revenue income**

The reason for making the distinction between these two types of classification is to ensure that the accounting system shows the true financial position for the business.

capital expenditure

Capital expenditure is expenditure incurred on the purchase, alteration or improvement of non-current (fixed) assets. You will remember (from Chapter 8) that non-current assets are items purchased by a business for use on a long-term basis.

Included in capital expenditure are such costs as:

- delivery of non-current assets
- installation of non-current assets
- improvement (but not repair) of non-current assets
- legal costs of buying property

An example of capital expenditure is the purchase of a car for use in the business.

Note that we use the word 'capitalised' to mean that an item has been treated as capital expenditure.

revenue expenditure

Revenue expenditure is expenditure incurred on purchases made by the business and on running expenses.

Included in revenue expenditure are the costs of:

- purchases made by the business
- maintenance and repair of non-current assets owned by the business
- administration of the business
- selling and distributing the goods or products in which the business trades

An example of revenue expenditure is the cost of petrol or diesel for the car used in the business.

capital expenditure and revenue expenditure – the differences

In the book-keeping system, it is important to classify correctly capital expenditure and revenue expenditure. An error in the double-entry book-keeping may show a false financial position for the business. For example, if the cost of the car was shown as an expense instead of as a non-current asset, the business will show a large motoring expense during the year but will not record that it owns the car as a non-current asset: in other words, the accounts will show an incorrect picture of the business.

Study the following examples: they show the differences between capital expenditure and revenue expenditure.

- **£30,000 cost of building an extension to the factory, which includes £1,000 for repairs to the existing factory**
  - capital expenditure £29,000
  - revenue expenditure £1,000 (because it is for repairs to an existing non-current asset)

- **a plot of land has been bought for £20,000, the legal costs are £750**
  - capital expenditure £20,750 (the legal costs are included in the capital expenditure, because they are the cost of acquiring the non-current asset, ie the legal costs are 'capitalised')

- **the business' own employees are used to install a new air conditioning system: wages £1,000, materials £1,500**
  - capital expenditure £2,500 (an addition to the property); note that, in cases such as this, the amounts for revenue expenditure, ie wages and materials purchases, will need to be reduced to allow for the transfer to capital expenditure

- **own employees used to repair and redecorate the premises: wages £500, materials £750**
  - revenue expenditure £1,250 (repairs and redecoration are running expenses)

- **purchase of a new machine £10,000, payment for installation and setting up £250**
  - capital expenditure, £10,250 (costs of installation of a non-current asset are capitalised)

Only by recording capital expenditure and revenue expenditure correctly in the double-entry book-keeping system can the business know the correct expenses amount and the correct amount of non-current assets it owns.

capital income

Capital income is income received from non-regular ('one-off') transactions.

Included in capital income are receipts from:

* sales of non-current assets

* loans raised from banks and other lenders

* capital, or increases in capital, paid in by the owner of the business

revenue income

Revenue income is income received from sales made by the business and other regular amounts of income.

Included in revenue income are the receipts from:

* sales made by the business

* rent from business premises rented out

* commission for work done by the business on behalf of other businesses

* cash discount for prompt settlement of amounts due to suppliers

recording capital income and revenue income

As with capital and revenue expenditure it is important to record capital income and revenue income correctly in the double-entry book-keeping system so as not to show a false financial position. For example, if the money received from the sale of a non-current asset was shown as income from sales it would increase the sales figure and, at the same time, there would be no record against the non-current asset of the amount it was sold for.

Chapter Summary

- The traditional 'T' account needs to be balanced at regular intervals – often the month-end.

- The 'balance b/d' is the account balance at the start of the next period.

- The balance of an account tells us information such as the amounts of sales, purchases, expenses to date, together with amounts of assets and liabilities.

- The accounting equation is another way of understanding double-entry book-keeping. It shows how the dual aspect of book-keeping relates to the accounts.

- The accounting equation always balances.

- Expenditure is classified between capital expenditure and revenue expenditure.

- Income is classified between capital income and revenue income.

- In the book-keeping system, it is important to classify capital and revenue expenditure and income correctly so as not to show a false position.

Key Terms

accounting equation	assets – liabilities = capital
assets	items owned by the business
liabilities	amounts owed by the business
capital	money invested in the business by the owner
capital expenditure	expenditure incurred on the purchase, alteration or improvement of non-current assets
revenue expenditure	expenditure incurred on purchases made by the business and on running expenses
capital income	income received from non-regular transactions
revenue income	income received from sales made by the business and other regular amounts of income

Activities

10.1 Balance the following accounts at 30 April 20-5, bringing down the balances on 1 May (a blank ledger account form can be downloaded from www.osbornebooks.co.uk):

Dr			Sales Account			Cr
20-5			£	20-5		£
				1 Apr	Balance b/d	12,555
				30 Apr	Sales Day Book	4,640

Dr			Sales Returns Account			Cr
20-5			£	20-5		£
1 Apr	Balance b/d		527			
30 Apr	Sales Returns Day Book		200			

Dr			Value Added Tax Account			Cr
20-5			£	20-5		£
30 Apr	Sales Returns Day Book		35	1 Apr	Balance b/d	1,233
				30 Apr	Sales Day Book	812

Dr			Wages Account			Cr
20-5			£	20-5		£
1 Apr	Balance b/d		6,045			
5 Apr	Bank		1,220			
26 Apr	Bank		2,165			

Dr			Doyle Traders			Cr
20-5			£	20-5		£
1 Apr	Balance b/d		183	14 Apr	Sales Returns	47
8 Apr	Sales		221			
22 Apr	Sales		395			

10.2 Balance the following accounts at 30 November 20-6, bringing down the balance on 1 December (a blank ledger account form can be downloaded from www.osbornebooks.co.uk):

Dr		Purchases Account			Cr
20-6		£	20-6		£
1 Nov	Balance b/d	64,287			
30 Nov	Purchases Day Book	6,720			

Dr		Purchases Returns Account			Cr
20-6		£	20-6		£
			1 Nov	Balance b/d	1,349
			30 Nov	Purchases Returns Day Book	160

Dr		Value Added Tax Account			Cr
20-6		£	20-6		£
30 Nov	Purchases Day Book	1,176	1 Nov	Balance b/d	644
			30 Nov	Purchases Returns Day Book	28

Dr		Rent Received Account			Cr
20-6		£	20-6		£
			1 Nov	Balance b/d	3,750
			14 Nov	Bank	375
			28 Nov	Bank	375

Dr		Murray Limited			Cr
20-6		£	20-6		£
1 Nov	Balance b/d	15	8 Nov	Purchases	230
11 Nov	Purchases Returns	42	16 Nov	Purchases	315
			24 Nov	Purchases	171

10.3 Show the double-entry, as it affects the accounting equation (assets – liabilities = capital), of the following sequence of transactions for a particular business:

- owner starts in business with capital of £8,000 in the bank
- buys a computer for £4,000, paying from the bank
- obtains a loan from a friend of £3,000, which is paid into the bank
- buys a van for £6,000, paying from the bank

10.4 Fill in the missing figures:

Assets	Liabilities	Capital
£	£	£
20,000	0	....
15,000	5,000	....
16,400	....	8,850
....	3,850	10,250
25,380	....	6,950
....	7,910	13,250

10.5 The table below sets out account balances from the books of a business. The opening capital is £10,000 which has been paid into the business bank account.

The columns (a) to (f) show the account balances resulting from a series of financial transactions that have taken place over time.

You are to compare each set of adjacent columns, ie (a) with (b), (b) with (c), and so on and state, with figures, what financial transactions have taken place in each case. The first has been completed for you.

Ignore VAT.

	(a)	(b)	(c)	(d)	(e)	(f)
	£	£	£	£	£	£
Assets						
Office equipment	–	2,000	2,000	2,000	2,000	2,000
Van	–	–	–	10,000	10,000	10,000
Bank	10,000	8,000	14,000	4,000	6,000	3,000
Liabilities						
Loan	–	–	6,000	6,000	6,000	3,000
Capital	10,000	10,000	10,000	10,000	12,000	12,000

Answer (a) - (b): Office equipment has been bought for £2,000 and paid from the bank.

10.6 Classify the following as either *capital expenditure* or *revenue expenditure* by putting a tick in the relevant column of the table below.

	CAPITAL EXPENDITURE	REVENUE EXPENDITURE
(a) purchase cost of vehicles		
(b) rent paid on premises		
(c) payments for purchases		
(d) legal fees paid relating to the purchase of property		
(e) cost of redecoration of the office		
(f) cost of installation of air-conditioning in the office		
(g) wages cost of own employees used to build extension to the stockroom		
(h) cost of installation and setting up of a new machine		

10.7 Classify the following as either *capital income* or *revenue income* by putting a tick in the relevant column of the table below.

	CAPITAL INCOME	REVENUE INCOME
(a) rent received		
(b) commission received		
(c) receipt from sale of old office equipment		
(d) bank loan received		
(e) receipts from sales		
(f) cash discount received		
(g) receipt from increase in owner's capital		
(h) receipt from sale of property		

11 The initial trial balance

this chapter covers...

We have already seen how it is necessary to balance the traditional form of account (the 'T' account) from time-to-time, according to the needs of the business.

In this chapter we list in two columns the balance of each account from the ledger, distinguishing between those accounts which have debit balances and those which have credit balances.

These two columns of debit and credit balances form the initial trial balance.

The two columns are totalled and if the two totals are the same, it proves that the accounting records are arithmetically correct.

If the two totals are not the same, it shows that there is an error, either in the addition of the columns or in the double-entry book-keeping.

This error should be traced and corrected.

This chapter shows how to prepare a trial balance manually. Many accounting systems use computer accounting, where the computer prints out a trial balance, in which case the totals should agree.

BALANCING THE ACCOUNTS

Before an initial trial balance can be extracted, it is necessary to balance each account in the general ledger. The balance brought down needs to be calculated correctly and shown on the correct side of the account. It is the balance brought down figure that is used in the initial trial balance.

Before moving on to the initial trial balance, do make sure that you are able to balance accounts accurately – please refer back to the previous chapter if you wish to review this process.

PREPARING AN INITIAL TRIAL BALANCE

An initial trial balance is prepared – or extracted – from the accounting records in order to make an initial check of the arithmetical accuracy of the double-entry book-keeping, ie that the debit entries equal the credit entries.

A trial balance is a list of the balances of every account from general ledger (including cash book and petty cash book), distinguishing between those accounts which have debit balances and those which have credit balances.

A trial balance is prepared at regular intervals – often at the end of each month – and the balances are set out in two totalled columns, a debit column and a credit column.

Read the three bullet point notes set out below and refer at the same time to the example trial balance shown on the next page.

- The debit and credit columns are totalled and the totals should agree. In this way the trial balance proves that the accounting records are arithmetically correct.
- The balance for each account listed in the trial balance is the amount brought down after the accounts have been balanced.
- As well as the name of each account, it is quite usual to show in the trial balance the account number. Most accounting systems give numbers to accounts and these can be listed in a separate 'reference' column. For sake of simplicity these details are not shown here.

Trial balance of Ace Suppliers as at 31 January 20-4

Account name	Debit £	Credit £
Purchases	7,500	
Sales		16,000
Sales returns	250	
Purchases returns		500
Sales ledger control	1,550	
Purchases ledger control		900
Rent	1,000	
Wages	1,500	
Heating and lighting	1,250	
Office equipment	5,000	
Machinery	7,500	
Inventory (Stock) at 1 Jan 20-4	2,500	
Petty cash	200	
Bank	4,850	
Value Added Tax		1,200
J Williams: loan		7,000
Capital		10,000
Drawings	2,500	
	35,600	35,600

a note about the asset of inventory (stock)

We have seen in earlier chapters how businesses use separate purchases and sales accounts to record when the goods in which they trade are bought and sold. The reason for using separate accounts for purchases and sales is because there is usually a difference between the buying price and the selling price – the latter is higher and gives the business its profit. At least once a year, however, a business values the inventory it has on the shelves of the shop, for example, or in the warehouse. As inventory is an asset of a business, the valuation is recorded as a debit to inventory account. This means that there will – for most businesses – be a debit balance on inventory account representing the value of inventory held at the beginning of the financial year. This balance will continue until such time as the inventory is formally valued again – often at the end of the financial year.

The debit balance for inventory is shown in the trial balance, as seen above.

DEBIT AND CREDIT BALANCES – GUIDELINES

Certain accounts always have a debit balance, while others always have a credit balance.

The lists set out below act as a guide, and will also help in your understanding of the initial trial balance.

debit balances

Debit balances are assets and expenses, and include:

- purchases account
- sales returns account
- fixed asset accounts, eg premises, motor vehicles, machinery, office equipment, etc
- inventory account – the inventory valuation, usually at the beginning of the year
- expenses accounts, eg wages, telephone, rent, etc
- drawings account
- sales ledger control account
- petty cash control account

credit balances

Credit balances are liabilities, income and capital, and include:

- sales account
- purchases returns account
- income accounts, eg rent received, commission received, fees received
- capital account
- loan account
- purchases ledger control account

Notes:
- **Bank control account** can be either debit or credit – it will be:
  - debit when the business has money in the bank
  - credit when it is overdrawn.
- **Value Added Tax account** can be either debit or credit – it will be:
  - debit when VAT is due to the business
  - credit when the business owes VAT to HM Revenue and Customs.

IF THE INITIAL TRIAL BALANCE DOESN'T BALANCE . . .

If the initial trial balance fails to balance, ie the two totals are different, there is an error (or errors):

- *either* in the addition of the trial balance
- *and/or* in the double-entry book-keeping

how to find an error

The procedure for finding the error(s) is as follows:

- check the addition of the trial balance
- check that the balance of each account has been correctly entered in the trial balance, and under the correct heading, ie debit or credit
- check that the balance of every account in general ledger has been included in the trial balance, together with the balance of cash book and petty cash book
- check that analysis columns from the cash book (for settlement discount and VAT), and from the petty cash book (for VAT and expenses) have been entered to the general ledger accounts
- check the calculation of the balance on each account
- calculate the amount that the trial balance is wrong, and then look in the accounts for a transaction for this amount: if one is found, check that the double-entry book-keeping has been carried out correctly
- halve the amount by which the trial balance is wrong, and look for a transaction for this amount: if it is found, check the double-entry book-keeping
- if the amount by which the trial balance is wrong is divisible by nine, then the error may be a reversal of figures, eg £65 entered as £56, or £45 entered as £54
- if the trial balance is wrong by a round amount, eg £10, £100, £1,000, the error is likely to be in the calculation of the account balances
- if the error(s) is still not found, it is necessary to check the book-keeping transactions since the date of the last trial balance, by going back to the financial documents and books of prime entry

The accounts supervisor needs to be informed if the trial balance still does not balance; he or she will give guidance as to what is to be done.

The Case Study that follows shows how an initial trial balance is constructed from a list of account balances.

Case Study

INITIAL TRIAL BALANCE

situation

You work as an accounts assistant for Severn Valley Stationery. The company sells office products and equipment to businesses in its area.

Today the accounts supervisor has asked you to work on preparing an initial trial balance as at 30 April 20-4. The supervisor has given you the following list of balances to be transferred to the trial balance.

You are to place the figures in the debit or credit column, as appropriate, and to total the debit and credit columns.

Account name	Amount £	Debit £	Credit £
Vehicles	20,500		
Inventory (Stock)	11,945		
Bank overdraft	8,297		
Petty cash control	110		
Sales ledger control	28,368		
Purchases ledger control	12,591		
VAT owing to HM Revenue & Customs	2,084		
Capital	23,237		
Loan from bank	20,500		
Sales	84,837		
Sales returns	1,089		
Purchases	51,054		
Purchases returns	2,210		
Discount allowed	105		
Discount received	215		
Vehicle expenses	3,175		
Wages	22,864		
Rent and rates	8,210		
Advertising	2,174		
Heating and lighting	968		
Travel costs	1,476		
Telephone	732		
Postages	591		
Miscellaneous expenses	610		
Totals	–		

solution

You take each balance in turn and enter it in either the debit balance column or the credit balance column.

You use the following guidelines:

DEBIT BALANCES (to go in the debit column)	CREDIT BALANCES (to go in the credit column)
• purchases	• sales
• sales returns	• purchases returns
• expenses (including discount allowed)	• income (including discount received)
• inventory (stock)	• capital
• sales ledger control	• purchases ledger control
• VAT (when refund is due from HM Revenue & Customs)	• VAT (when owed to HM Revenue & Customs)
• bank (money in bank)	• bank overdraft
• petty cash control	• loan/bank loan
• non-current (fixed) assets	
• drawings	

When you have entered the balances in the appropriate column, you then total the two columns of the trial balance – if the debit and credit totals are the same, this proves that the accounting records are arithmetically correct. If the trial balance doesn't balance, you follow the procedures for finding error(s) along the lines of those set out on page 210.

The initial trial balance of Severn Valley Stationery as at 30 April 20-4 then appears as shown on the next page.

Account name	Amount £	Debit £	Credit £
Vehicles	20,500	20,500	
Inventory (Stock)	11,945	11,945	
Bank overdraft	8,297		8,297
Petty cash control	110	110	
Sales ledger control	28,368	28,368	
Purchases ledger control	12,591		12,591
VAT owing to HM Revenue & Customs	2,084		2,084
Capital	23,237		23,237
Loan from bank	20,500		20,500
Sales	84,837		84,837
Sales returns	1,089	1,089	
Purchases	51,054	51,054	
Purchases returns	2,210		2,210
Discount allowed	105	105	
Discount received	215		215
Vehicle expenses	3,175	3,175	
Wages	22,864	22,864	
Rent and rates	8,210	8,210	
Advertising	2,174	2,174	
Heating and lighting	968	968	
Travel costs	1,476	1,476	
Telephone	732	732	
Postages	591	591	
Miscellaneous expenses	610	610	
Totals	–	153,971	153,971

Note that the format of the initial trial balance shown above includes the original 'Amount' column to show you the process of transferring the account balances to the correct debit or credit column. In reality the initial trial balance is likely only to show the debit and credit money columns. It will also be headed up with the name of the business and the date of the trial balance.

The trial balance of Severn Valley Stationery is shown in its final form on the next page.

Severn Valley Stationery

Trial Balance as at 30 April 20-4

Account name	Debit £	Credit £
Vehicles	20,500	
Inventory (Stock)	11,945	
Bank overdraft		8,297
Petty cash control	110	
Sales ledger control	28,368	
Purchases ledger control		12,591
VAT owing to HM Revenue & Customs		2,084
Capital		23,237
Loan from bank		20,500
Sales		84,837
Sales returns	1,089	
Purchases		51,054
Purchases returns		2,210
Discount allowed	105	
Discount received		215
Vehicle expenses	3,175	
Wages	22,864	
Rent and rates	8,210	
Advertising	2,174	
Heating and lighting	968	
Travel costs	1,476	
Telephone	732	
Postages	591	
Miscellaneous expenses	610	
Totals	153,971	153,971

Chapter Summary

- An initial trial balance is prepared by taking the balances brought down of each account in the ledger and setting them out in debit and credit columns.

- Debit balances include accounts for purchases, sales returns, fixed assets, inventory, expenses, sales ledger control and petty cash control.

- Credit balances include accounts for sales, purchases returns, income, capital, loan and purchases ledger control.

- The balances of bank control account and VAT account can be either debit or credit – depending on the circumstances.

- In the initial trial balance the totals of the columns for debit and credit balances should be the same.

- The initial trial balance checks the arithmetical accuracy of the double-entry book-keeping, ie that the debit entries equal the credit entries.

- If the initial trial balance fails to balance, there is an error (or errors):
  - *either* in the addition of the trial balance
  - *and/or* in the double-entry book-keeping

- Any error (or errors) must be traced and corrected

Key Terms

initial trial balance	list of the balances of every account from general ledger (including cash book and petty cash book), distinguishing between those accounts which have debit balances and those which have credit balances
debit balances	include assets, expenses, drawings, purchases, sales returns
credit balances	include liabilities, income, capital, sales, purchases returns

Activities

11.1   Which one of the following accounts always has a debit balance?

(a)   capital account

(b)   purchases account

(c)   sales account

(d)   purchases returns account

Answer (a) or (b) or (c) or (d)

11.2   Which one of the following accounts always has a credit balance?

(a)   sales returns account

(b)   premises account

(c)   capital account

(d)   wages account

Answer (a) or (b) or (c) or (d)

11.3   Prepare the initial trial balance of Jane Greenwell as at 31 March 20-9. She has omitted to open a capital account. You are to fill in the missing figure in order to balance the trial balance.

	£
Bank overdraft	1,250
Purchases	850
Petty cash	48
Sales	1,940
Purchases returns	144
Payables (creditors)	1,442
Equipment	2,704
Van	3,200
Inventory (Stock) at 1 April 20-8	1,210
Sales returns	90
Receivables (debtors)	1,174
Wages	1,500
Capital	?

11.4 You work as an accounts assistant for Pershore Products. The accounts supervisor has asked you to work on preparing an initial trial balance as at 30 June 20-2. The supervisor has given you the following list of balances to be transferred to the trial balance.

You are to place the figures in the debit or credit column, as appropriate, and total the debit and credit columns.

Account name	Amount £	Debit £	Credit £
Office equipment	12,246		
Bank (debit balance)	3,091		
Petty cash control	84		
Inventory (Stock)	11,310		
Capital	22,823		
Drawings	2,550		
VAT owing to HM Revenue & Customs	3,105		
Loan from bank	8,290		
Purchases ledger control	17,386		
Sales ledger control	30,274		
Sales	82,410		
Purchases	39,496		
Purchases returns	2,216		
Sales returns	3,471		
Discount received	298		
Discount allowed	517		
Wages	20,212		
Advertising	4,390		
Insurance	1,045		
Heating and lighting	1,237		
Rent and rates	4,076		
Travel costs	854		
Postages	721		
Telephone	954		
Totals	–		

11.5 You work as an accounts assistant for Arley Limited. The accounts supervisor has asked you to work on preparing an initial trial balance as at 31 December 20-6. The supervisor has given you the following list of balances to be transferred to the trial balance.

You are to place the figures in the debit or credit column, as appropriate, and total the debit and credit columns.

Account name	Amount £	Debit £	Credit £
Sales	101,269		
Sales returns	3,476		
Purchases	54,822		
Purchases returns	4,107		
Sales ledger control	25,624		
Purchases ledger control	18,792		
Discount received	399		
Discount allowed	210		
Rent and rates	3,985		
Advertising	4,867		
Insurance	1,733		
Wages	31,246		
Heating and lighting	3,085		
Postages	1,211		
Telephone	985		
Travel costs	2,311		
Miscellaneous expenses	107		
Capital	22,489		
Vehicles	22,400		
Inventory (Stock)	12,454		
Petty cash control	85		
Bank overdraft	6,291		
VAT owing to HM Revenue & Customs	3,054		
Loan from bank	12,200		
Totals	–		

Answers to activities

CHAPTER 1: INTRODUCTION TO THE ACCOUNTING SYSTEM

1.1   (b)

1.2   True

1.3   (c)

1.4   (a)

1.5   (b)

1.6   (c)

1.7   (c)

1.8   (a)

1.9   (a)   £10,500

     (b)   £6,720

     (c)   £3,000

     (d)   £155,000

     (e)   sales ledger and purchases ledger control accounts

CHAPTER 2: FINANCIAL DOCUMENTS FOR SALES

2.1   (a)   delivery note   (b)   invoice

     (c)   statement   (d)   credit note   (e)   purchase order

2.2   (a)   the percentage allowance given to customers who regularly deal with the seller.

     (b)   £159.50 - £47.85 discount = £111.65 plus VAT of £19.53 (rounded down) = £131.18

2.3

	total	discount	net total	VAT	invoice total
	£	£	£	£	£
(a)	160.00	32.00	128.00	22.40	150.40
(b)	400.00	80.00	320.00	56.00	376.00
(c)	40.00	none	40.00	7.00	47.00
(d)	8000.00	1600.00	6400.00	1120.00	7520.00

2.4

	net total	discount deducted	total after cash discount	VAT	invoice total*
(a)	128.00	3.20	124.80	21.84	149.84
(b)	320.00	8.00	312.00	54.60	374.60
(c)	40.00	1.00	39.00	6.82	46.82
(d)	6400.00	160.00	6240.00	1092.00	7492.00

*Remember that the VAT is normally added to the total before deduction of cash discount.

2.5   The problems are the urgency and the need for accuracy. If the wrong goods are sent the problems will be compounded.

Solutions: telephone or e-mail, and fax a copy of the order pointing out the error.

Best and quickest solution – telephone.

Important point – ask for a replacement corrected order to be sent (marked 'confirmation' to avoid duplication), so that a further check can be made. This is to make sure your position is strong, just in case the customer gets it wrong again! This type of problem can be sorted out at assistant level, but should be reported to the line manager when he/she returns.

2.6   Examples: Purchase order number, delivery note number, invoice number, inventory code, account number, credit note number.
The main importance of coding is for accurate cross referencing. It is also important for efficient filing.

2.7   (b)

2.8   (a)   Incorrect discount rate applied (10%), wrong addition for total. Goods total should be £76.00, VAT £13.30 and final total £89.30.

(b)   Total before discount should be £250.00. VAT has also been rounded up (should have been rounded down to £35.43). Corrected figures: goods total £225.00 (after deduction of 10% discount), VAT £39.37, final total £264.37.

2.9   Statement should be dated 31 July 20-3 and addressed to Mr Simpson.
The entries are:

20-3		debit £	credit £	balance £
1 July	Balance b/f	58.75		58.75
4 July	Cheque received		58.75	00.00
8 July	Invoice 10982	340.75		340.75
14 July	Credit note 2378		34.07	306.68
			TOTAL	306.68

CHAPTER 3: ACCOUNTING FOR SALES AND SALES RETURNS

3.1 (a)

3.2 (a)

3.3 (a) • The financial documents for credit sales transactions are sales invoices that have been checked and authorised.

 • The details and amounts of the invoices are entered into sales day book. In the money columns of sales day book is recorded:

 – total column, the final total of each invoice

 – VAT column, the VAT amount shown on each invoice

 – net column, the net ('goods or services total') amount of each invoice

 • After sales day book has been written up for the week or month, it is totalled and the information from it is transferred into the double-entry system.

 • The book-keeping entries are:

 – the total of the total column is debited to sales ledger control account in general ledger

 – the total of the VAT column is credited to VAT account in general ledger

 – the total of the net column is credited to sales account in general ledger

 – the amounts from the total column for each separate transaction are debited to the memorandum accounts of the customers in sales ledger

 (b) • The financial documents for sales returns transactions are credit notes issued that have been checked and authorised.

 • The details and amounts of the credit notes are entered into sales returns day book. In the money columns of the sales returns day book is recorded:

 – total column, the final total of each credit note

 – VAT column, the VAT amount shown on each credit note

 – net column, the net ('goods or services total') amount of each credit note

 • After sales returns day book has been written up for the week or month, it is totalled and the information from it is transferred into the double-entry system.

 • The book-keeping entries are:

 – the total of the total column is credited to sales ledger control account in general ledger

 – the total of the VAT column is debited to VAT account in general ledger

 – the total of the net column is debited to sales returns account in general ledger

 – the amounts from the total column for each separate transaction are credited to the memorandum accounts of the customers in sales ledger

3.4 (a)

Sales Day Book						SDB50
Date	Details	Invoice number	Reference	Total	VAT	Net
20-5				£ p	£ p	£ p
2 Apr	Malvern Stores	4578	SL110	64.62	9.62	55.00
5 Apr	Pershore Retailers	4579	SL145	76.37	11.37	65.00
7 Apr	E Grainger	4580	SL055	32.90	4.90	28.00
9 Apr	P Wilson	4581	SL172	68.15	10.15	58.00
12 Apr	M Kershaw	4582	SL090	89.30	13.30	76.00
14 Apr	D Lloyd	4583	SL095	77.55	11.55	66.00
19 Apr	A Cox	4584	SL032	38.77	5.77	33.00
22 Apr	Dines Stores	4585	SL048	119.85	17.85	102.00
23 Apr	Malvern Stores	4586	SL110	55.22	8.22	47.00
26 Apr	P Wilson	4587	SL172	41.12	6.12	35.00
29 Apr	A Cox	4588	SL032	96.35	14.35	82.00
30 Apr	Totals for month			760.20	113.20	647.00
				GL1200	GL2200	GL4100

(b)

GENERAL LEDGER

Dr	**Sales Ledger Control Account** (GL1200)			Cr
20-5		£ p	20-5	£ p
30 Apr Sales Day Book SDB50		760.20		

Dr	**Value Added Tax Account** (GL2200)			Cr
20-5		£ p	20-5	£ p
			30 Apr Sales Day Book SDB50	113.20

Dr	**Sales Account** (GL4100)			Cr
20-5		£ p	20-5	£ p
			30 Apr Sales Day Book SDB50	647.00

SALES LEDGER

Dr	**Malvern Stores** (SL110)				Cr
20-5			£ p	20-5	£ p
2 Apr	Sales	SDB50	64.62		
23 Apr	Sales	SDB50	55.22		

Dr	**Pershore Retailers** (SL145)				Cr
20-5			£ p	20-5	£ p
5 Apr	Sales	SDB50	76.37		

Dr			**E Grainger** (SL055)			Cr
20-5			£ p	20-5		£ p
7 Apr	Sales	SDB50	32.90			

Dr			**P Wilson** (SL172)			Cr
20-5			£ p	20-5		£ p
9 Apr	Sales	SDB50	68.15			
26 Apr	Sales	SDB50	41.12			

Dr			**M Kershaw** (SL090)			Cr
20-5			£ p	20-5		£ p
12 Apr	Sales	SDB50	89.30			

Dr			**D Lloyd** (SL095)			Cr
20-5			£ p	20-5		£ p
14 Apr	Sales	SDB 50	77.55			

Dr			**A Cox** (SL032)			Cr
20-5			£ p	20-5		£ p
19 Apr	Sales	SDB 50	38.77			
29 Apr	Sales	SDB 50	96.35			

Dr			**Dines Stores** (SL048)			Cr
20-5			£ p	20-5		£ p
22 Apr	Sales	SDB 50	119.85			

3.5   (a)

Sales Returns Day Book					SRDB18	
Date	Details	Credit note no	Reference	Total	VAT	Net
20-5				£ p	£ p	£ p
8 Apr	Pershore Retailers	572	SL145	23.50	3.50	20.00
12 Apr	E Grainger	573	SL055	32.90	4.90	28.00
16 Apr	D Lloyd	574	SL095	38.77	5.77	33.00
28 Apr	Malvern Stores	575	SL110	23.50	3.50	20.00
30 Apr	A Cox	576	SL032	47.00	7.00	40.00
30 Apr	Totals for month			165.67	24.67	141.00
				GL1200	GL2200	GL4110

(b)

GENERAL LEDGER

Dr		Sales Ledger Control Account (GL1200)				Cr
20-5			£ p	20-5		£ p
30 Apr	Sales Day Book	SDB50	760.20	30 Apr Sales Returns Day Book	SRDB18	165.67

Dr		Value Added Tax Account (GL2200)				Cr
20-5			£ p	20-5		£ p
30 Apr	Sales Returns Day Book	SRDB18	24.67	30 Apr Sales Day Book	SDB50	113.20

Dr		Sales Returns Account (GL4110)			Cr
20-5			£ p	20-5	£ p
30 Apr	Sales Returns Day Book	SRDB18	141.00		

SALES LEDGER

Dr		Pershore Retailers (SL145)					Cr
20-5			£ p	20-5			£ p
5 Apr	Sales	SDB50	76.37	8 Apr	Sales Returns	SRDB18	23.50

Dr		E Grainger (SL055)					Cr
20-5			£ p	20-5			£ p
7 Apr	Sales	SDB50	32.90	12 Apr	Sales Returns	SRDB18	32.90

Dr		D Lloyd (SL095)					Cr
20-5			£ p	20-5			£ p
14 Apr	Sales	SDB50	77.55	16 Apr	Sales Returns	SRDB18	38.77

Dr		Malvern Stores (SL110)					Cr
20-5			£ p	20-5			£ p
2 Apr	Sales	SDB50	64.62	28 Apr	Sales Returns	SRDB18	23.50
23 Apr	Sales	SDB50	55.22				

Dr		A Cox (SL032)					Cr
20-5			£ p	20-5			£ p
19 Apr	Sales	SDB50	38.77	30 Apr	Sales Returns	SRDB18	47.00
29 Apr	Sales	SDB50	96.35				

3.6 (a)

General ledger

Account name	Amount £	Debit ✓	Credit ✓
Sales	10,600		✓
Value Added Tax	1,855		✓
Sales ledger control	12,455	✓	

Sales ledger

Account name	Amount £	Debit ✓	Credit ✓
Bowne Ltd	940	✓	
Jamieson & Co	4,841	✓	
Pottertons	3,807	✓	
Wells plc	2,867	✓	

(b)

General ledger

Account name	Amount £	Debit ✓	Credit ✓
Sales returns	1,520	✓	
Value Added Tax	266	✓	
Sales ledger control	1,786		✓

Sales ledger

Account name	Amount £	Debit ✓	Credit ✓
Lloyd & Co	564		✓
Wyvern Stores	1,222		✓

3.7

Customer	Sales ledger account code
Dymock Trading Co	DYM003
Hedgehog Fashions	HED001
Jones & Co	JON002

Note: Dymock Trading Co is numbered '003' because an '002' account number has been allocated already for 'D'; similarly for Jones & Co where '001' has been allocated already for 'J'.

CHAPTER 4: PROCESS PAYMENTS FROM CUSTOMERS

4.1   (d)

4.2   (b)

4.3   (a)   The remittance advice does not take account of the credit note issued on 10 November and so includes an overpayment of £49.00. Cool Socks should advise the customer, Trends, of this discrepancy and suggest that an adjustment could be made when the next month's payment is due, the credit remaining on the account for the time being.

   (b)   The remittance advice does not include payment of an invoice for £625.85 issued on 17 November and so the discrepancy is an underpayment. As the amount is large, Cool Socks should contact Vogue Limited and ask for payment. If the invoice is disputed, the problem should be looked into and resolved as soon as possible.

   (c)   RTC Fashions have underpaid their account because they have deducted 5% settlement discount when it was not offered (it is not included in the terms on the Chico Importers invoice). Additionally they have adjusted and underpaid the VAT by £4.90. Chico Importers should either ask RTC Fashions for payment of the shortfall of £32.90 immediately or advise them of the problem and suggest that an adjustment could be made when the next month's payment is due, the debit remaining on RTC Fashions' account for the time being. The decision depends on the relationship that exists between the supplier and customer.

CHAPTER 5: PROCESS DOCUMENTS FROM SUPPLIERS

5.1   (a)   purchase order

        (b)   delivery note

        (c)   goods received note

        (d)   invoice

        (e)   credit note

5.2   A delivery note is sent by the seller with the goods, a goods received note is an internal document used by the purchaser to record and action any discrepancies found when the goods arrive.

5.3   (a)

5.4   Credit note.

5.5   The errors are:

        (a)   the goods were delivered to the wrong address

        (b)   an incorrect customer discount has been applied (10% instead of 15%)

        (c)   the wrong goods were sent (product code 4574 instead of 4573)

    The total should have been £95 less 15% discount = £80.75 plus VAT of £14.13 = £94.88

    The email should point out these errors and state that the disks are being returned for credit.

5.6   (a)   Errors on credit note:

           – Wrong reference - should be 17643

           – Product code incorrect – should be 919BK

           – Should be gel pens, not rollerball pens

           – credit should be for 2 boxes, not 3

           – discount deducted at 20%, should be 10%, making net total £21.60, VAT £3.78, total £25.38.

        As the goods received are correct, the email should point out the errors on the credit note and ask for a revised document to be issued.

        (b)

supplier a/c reference	general ledger a/c number
HE001	5010

CHAPTER 6: ACCOUNTING FOR PURCHASES AND PURCHASES RETURNS

6.1   (c)

6.2   (d)

6.3   (b)

6.4   (a)   • The financial documents for credit purchases transactions are purchases invoices, received from suppliers, that have been checked and authorised.

   • The details and amounts of the invoices are entered into the purchases day book. In the money columns of purchases day book is recorded:

   – total column, the final total of each invoice

   – VAT column, the VAT amount shown on each invoice

   – net column, the net ('goods or services total') amount of each invoice

   • After purchases day book has been written up for the week or month, it is totalled and the information from it is transferred into the double-entry system.

   • The book-keeping entries are:

   – the total of the total column is credited to purchases ledger control account in general ledger

   – the total of the VAT column is debited to VAT account in general ledger

   – the total of the net column is debited to purchases account in general ledger

   – the amounts from the total column for each separate transaction are credited to the memorandum accounts of the suppliers in purchases ledger

(b)   • The financial documents for purchases returns transactions are credit notes, received from suppliers, that have been checked and authorised.

   • The details and amounts of the credit notes are entered into purchases returns day book. In the money columns of the purchases returns day book is recorded:

   – total column, the final total of each credit note

   – VAT column, the VAT amount shown on each credit note

   – net column, the net ('goods or services total') amount of each credit note

   • After purchases returns day book has been written up for the week or month, it is totalled and the information from it is transferred into the double-entry system.

   • The book-keeping entries are:

   – the total of the total column is debited to purchases ledger control account in general ledger

   – the total of the VAT column is credited to VAT account in general ledger

   – the total of the net column is credited to purchases returns account in general ledger

   – the amounts from the total column for each separate transaction are debited to the memorandum accounts of the suppliers in purchases ledger

6.5   (a)

Purchases Day Book						PDB36
Date	Details	Invoice number	Reference	Total	VAT	Net
20-5				£ p	£ p	£ p
2 Apr	Severn Supplies	6789	PL721	293.75	43.75	250.00
5 Apr	I Johnstone	A241	PL604	246.75	36.75	210.00
9 Apr	L Murphy	2456	PL659	217.37	32.37	185.00
15 Apr	Mercia Manufacturing	X457	PL627	211.50	31.50	180.00
19 Apr	AMC Enterprises	AMC 456	PL520	405.37	60.37	345.00
26 Apr	S Green	2846	PL574	464.12	69.12	395.00
30 Apr	Totals for month			1,838.86	273.86	1,565.00
				GL2350	GL2200	GL5100

(b)   **GENERAL LEDGER**

Dr   **Value Added Tax Account** (GL2200)   Cr

20-5			£ p	20-5			£ p
30 Apr	Purchases Day Book	PDB36	273.86				

Dr   **Purchases Ledger Control Account** (GL2350)   Cr

20-5			£ p	20-5			£ p
				30 Apr	Purchases Day Book	PDB36	1,838.86

Dr   **Purchases Account** (GL5100)   Cr

20-5			£ p	20-5			£ p
30 Apr	Purchases Day Book	PDB36	1,565.00				

PURCHASES LEDGER

Dr   **Severn Supplies** (PL721)   Cr

20-5			£ p	20-5			£ p
				2 Apr	Purchases	PDB36	293.75

Dr   **I Johnstone** (PL604)   Cr

20-5			£ p	20-5			£ p
				5 Apr	Purchases	PDB36	246.75

Dr			**L Murphy** (PL659)			Cr
20-5		£ p	20-5			£ p
			9 Apr	Purchases	PDB36	217.37

Dr			**Mercia Manufacturing** (PL627)			Cr
20-5		£ p	20-5			£ p
			15 Apr	Purchases	PDB36	211.50

Dr			**AMC Enterprises** (PL520)			Cr
20-5		£ p	20-5			£ p
			19 Apr	Purchases	PDB36	405.37

Dr			**S Green** (PL574)			Cr
20-5		£ p	20-5			£ p
			26 Apr	Purchases	PDB36	464.12

6.6 (a)

	Purchases Returns Day Book					PRDB11
Date	Details	Credit note no	Reference	Total	VAT	Net
20-5				£ p	£ p	£ p
7 Apr	Severn Supplies	225	PL 721	58.75	8.75	50.00
14 Apr	L Murphy	X456	PL 659	94.00	14.00	80.00
21 Apr	AMC Enterprises	3921	PL 520	146.87	21.87	125.00
29 Apr	S Green	SG247	PL 574	79.90	11.90	68.00
30 Apr	Totals for month			379.52	56.52	323.00
				GL2350	GL2200	GL5110

(b)

GENERAL LEDGER

Dr		**Value Added Tax Account** (GL2200)			Cr
20-5		£ p	20-5		£ p
30 Apr	Purchases Day Book PDB36	273.86	30 Apr	Purchases Returns Day Book PRDB11	56.52

Dr		**Purchases Ledger Control Account** (GL2350)			Cr
20-5		£ p	20-5		£ p
30 Apr	Purchases Returns Day Book PRDB11	379.52	30 Apr	Purchases Day Book PDB36	1,838.86

Dr   **Purchases Returns Account** (GL5110)   Cr

20-5	£ p	20-5		£ p
		30 Apr Purchases Returns Day Book	PRDB11	323.00

PURCHASES LEDGER

Dr   **Severn Supplies** (PL721)   Cr

20-5		£ p	20-5		£ p
7 Apr Purchases Returns	PRDB11	58.75	2 Apr Purchases	PDB36	293.75

Dr   **L Murphy** (PL659)   Cr

20-5		£ p	20-5		£ p
14 Apr Purchases Returns	PRDB11	94.00	9 Apr Purchases	PDB36	217.37

Dr   **AMC Enterprises** (PL520)   Cr

20-5		£ p	20-5		£ p
21 Apr Purchases Returns	PRDB11	146.87	19 Apr Purchases	PDB36	405.37

Dr   **S Green** (PL574)   Cr

20-5		£ p	20-5		£ p
29 Apr Purchases Returns	PRDB11	79.90	26 Apr Purchases	PDB36	464.12

6.7 (a)

General ledger

Account name	Amount £	Debit ✓	Credit ✓
Purchases	8,040	✓	
Value Added Tax	1,407	✓	
Purchases ledger control	9,447		✓

Purchases ledger

Account name	Amount £	Debit ✓	Credit ✓
Seng Ltd	1,128		✓
Peall & Co	2,773		✓
Knightons	4,089		✓
Galeazzi plc	1,457		✓

(b)

General ledger

Account name	Amount £	Debit ✓	Credit ✓
Purchases returns	1,440		✓
Value Added Tax	252		✓
Purchases ledger control	1,692	✓	

Purchases ledger

Account name	Amount £	Debit ✓	Credit ✓
Martin & Co	1,034	✓	
Wentworth Stores	658	✓	

6.8

Supplier	Purchases ledger account code
Bridon Ltd	BRI003
Foster & Co	FOS001
Hirst & Co	HIR002

Note: Bridon Ltd is numbered '003' because an '002' account number has been allocated already for 'B'; similarly for Hirst & Co where '001' has been allocated already for 'H'.

CHAPTER 7: PREPARE PAYMENTS TO SUPPLIERS

7.1   (c)

7.2   (a)

7.3   (b)

7.4   (c)

7.5   Invoice £150 on 8 March ref 76333 has been entered twice on the statement of account but only once in the purchases ledger. It is likely to be a duplication and should be queried with Luxon Traders. The likely outcome is a payment of £100 (invoice for £150 less credit note for £50).

7.6   Credit note £72.90 on 22 April appears in the purchases ledger but not on the supplier statement. Having checked that the credit note has been correctly posted to the purchases ledger account, you should query it with A Krauss Trading, as they may have posted it to the wrong account, or not posted it at all. The likely outcome is a payment of £269.85 (invoices for £233.25 and £109.50 less credit note for £72.90).

7.7

BACS REMITTANCE ADVICE		FROM: Hetherington Limited Unit 23 Wessex Estate Langborne Road Seatown SE8 5VZ	
TO Aldersgate Supplies 10 Aldersgate Street, London EC1A 7GH			
		date: 3 October 20-5	
date	your reference	our reference	payment amount £
08 09 20-5	Invoice 10945	PO85262	120.75
14 09 20-5	Invoice 10963	PO85271	380.25
20 09 20-5	Credit note 109	PO85248	(46.00)
		TOTAL	455.00

THIS AMOUNT HAS BEEN PAID BY BACS CREDIT TRANSFER DIRECTLY INTO YOUR BANK ACCOUNT AT ALBION BANK ACCOUNT NO 17643987 SORT CODE 99 43 83

7.8

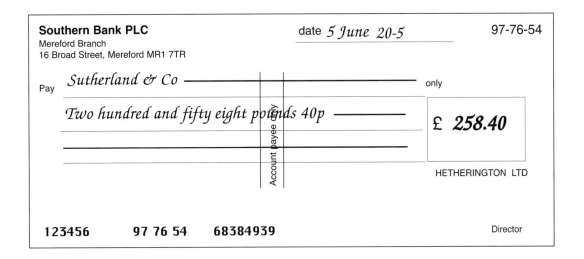

REMITTANCE ADVICE			FROM: Hetherington Limited Unit 23 Wessex Estate Langborne Road Seatown SE8 5VZ

TO Sutherland & Co
     67 Great March Street
     Eastwick, EA3 9JN

date: 5 June 20-5

date	your reference	our reference	payment amount £
23 May 20-5	Invoice 7856	472984	345.90
29 May 20-5	Credit note 4562	472975	(87.50)
		CHEQUE TOTAL	258.40

Southern Bank PLC
Mereford Branch
16 Broad Street, Mereford MR1 7TR

date *5 June 20-5*   97-76-54

Pay *Sutherland & Co* —————————— only

Two hundred and fifty eight pounds 40p ————

Account payee

£ *258.40*

HETHERINGTON LTD

123456   97 76 54   68384939

Director

CHAPTER 8: CASH BOOK

8.1   (d)

8.2   (b)

8.3   GENERAL LEDGER

Dr   **Capital Account**   Cr
20-7			£	20-7			£
				30 Apr	Bank	CB70	8,000

Dr   **Bank: Loan Account**   Cr
20-7			£	20-7			£
				30 Apr	Bank	CB70	5,000

Dr   **Rent Account**   Cr
20-7			£	20-7		£
30 Apr	Bank	CB70	1,000			

Dr   **Wages Account**   Cr
20-7			£	20-7		£
30 Apr	Bank	CB70	800			

Dr   **Drawings Account**   Cr
20-7			£	20-7		£
30 Apr	Bank	CB70	500			

Dr   **Vehicles Account**   Cr
20-7			£	20-7		£
30 Apr	Bank	CB70	10,000			

8.4   (a)

Sales ledger

Account name	Amount £	Debit ✓	Credit ✓
T Jones	2,750		✓

(b)

General ledger

Account name	Amount £	Debit ✓	Credit ✓
Sales	400		✓
Wages	1,175	✓	
Rent	1,200	✓	
Drawings	600	✓	
Bank: loan account	750	✓	
Sales ledger control	2,750		✓
VAT	70		✓

8.5 (a)   True

(b)   False – the balance b/d of £902 on 1 May shows that, according to the cash book, there is a bank overdraft.

(c)   **GENERAL LEDGER**

Dr		**Sales Account**			Cr
20-5		£	20-5		£
			30 Apr Bank	CB32	200

Dr		**Commission Received Account**			Cr
20-5		£	20-5		£
			30 Apr Bank	CB32	40

Dr		**Sales Ledger Control Account**			Cr
20-5		£	20-5		£
			30 Apr Bank	CB32	2,400
			30 Apr Discount allowed	CB32	40

Dr		**Bank: Loan Account**			Cr
20-5		£	20-5		£
			30 Apr Bank	CB32	2,000

Dr		**Purchases Ledger Control Account**			Cr
20-5		£	20-5		£
30 Apr Bank	CB32	3,200			
30 Apr Discount received	CB32	50			

Dr		Purchases Account		Cr	
20-5			£	20-5	£
30 Apr	Bank	CB32	80		

Dr		Office Equipment Account		Cr	
20-5			£	20-5	£
30 Apr	Bank	CB32	2,000		

Dr		Wages Account		Cr	
20-5			£	20-5	£
30 Apr	Bank	CB32	1,550		

Dr		General Expenses Account		Cr	
20-5			£	20-5	£
30 Apr	Bank	CB32	400		

Dr		Discount Allowed Account		Cr	
20-5			£	20-5	£
30 Apr	Bank	CB32	40		

Dr		Discount Received Account		Cr		
20-5			£	20-5		£
				30 Apr	Bank CB32	50

Dr		Value Added Tax Account		Cr		
20-5			£	20-5		£
30 April	Bank	CB32	434	30 Apr	Bank CB32	42

SALES LEDGER

Dr		Lindum Limited		Cr		
20-5			£	20-5		£
				30 Apr	Bank CB32	2,400
				30 Apr	Discount allowed CB32	40

PURCHASES LEDGER

Dr		Mereford Mills		Cr	
20-5			£	20-5	£
30 Apr	Bank	CB32	3,200		
30 Apr	Discount received	CB32	50		

8.6 (a)

CHAPTER 9: PETTY CASH BOOK

9.1   (c)

9.2   (a)

9.3

	✓
Debit	✓
Credit	

9.4   General ledger

Account name	Amount £	Debit ✓	Credit ✓
Petty cash book/Petty cash control account	75.00	✓	
Bank	75.00		✓

9.5   General ledger

Account name	Amount £	Debit ✓	Credit ✓
VAT	3.85	✓	
Postages	18.30	✓	
Travel	10.90	✓	
Meals	6.35	✓	
Office sundries	15.60	✓	
Bank	55.00		✓

9.6 (a)

GENERAL LEDGER

Dr		Value Added Tax Account					Cr
20-9			£	20-9			£
31 Mar	Petty cash book	PCB20	3.99				

Dr		Travel Account					Cr
20-9			£	20-9			£
31 Mar	Petty cash book	PCB20	24.26				

Dr		Postages Account					Cr
20-9			£	20-9			£
31 Mar	Petty cash book	PCB20	16.65	12 Mar	Petty cash book	PCB20	8.50

Dr		Stationery Account					Cr
20-9			£	20-9			£
31 Mar	Petty cash book	PCB20	9.60				

Dr		Meals Account					Cr
20-9			£	20-9			£
31 Mar	Petty cash book	PCB20	5.00				

Dr		Purchases Ledger Control Account					Cr
20-9			£	20-9			£
31 Mar	Petty cash book	PCB20	13.50				

Dr		Petty Cash Control Account					Cr
20-9			£	20-9			£
1 Mar	Balance b/d		100.00	31 Mar	Petty cash book	PCB20	73.00
31 Mar	Petty cash book	PCB20	8.50	31 Mar	Balance c/d		100.00
31 Mar	Bank	CB	64.50				
			173.00				173.00
1 Apr	Balance b/d		100.00				

Dr		Cash Book					Cr
20-9			Bank	20-9			Bank
				31 Mar	Petty cash	PCB20	64.50

(b)

PURCHASES LEDGER

Dr		P Andrews					Cr
20-9			£	20-9			£
31 Mar	Petty cash book	PCB20	13.50				

CHAPTER 10: BALANCING ACCOUNTS, THE ACCOUNTING EQUATION, CAPITAL AND REVENUE

10.1

Dr			Sales Account		Cr
20-5		£	20-5		£
30 Apr	Balance c/d	17,195	1 Apr	Balance b/d	12,555
			30 Apr	Sales Day Book	4,640
		17,195			17,195
			1 May	Balance b/d	17,195

Dr			Sales Returns Account		Cr
20-5		£	20-5		£
1 Apr	Balance b/d	527	30 Apr	Balance c/d	727
30 Apr	Sales Returns Day Book	200			
		727			727
1 May	Balance b/d	727			

Dr			Value Added Tax Account		Cr
20-5		£	20-5		£
30 Apr	Sales Returns Day Book	35	1 Apr	Balance b/d	1,233
30 Apr	Balance c/d	2,010	30 Apr	Sales Day Book	812
		2,045			2,045
			1 May	Balance b/d	2,010

Dr			Wages Account		Cr
20-5		£	20-5		£
1 Apr	Balance b/d	6,045	30 Apr	Balance c/d	9,430
5 Apr	Bank	1,220			
26 Apr	Bank	2,165			
		9,430			9,430
1 May	Balance b/d	9,430			

Dr			Doyle Traders		Cr
20-5		£	20-5		£
1 Apr	Balance b/d	183	14 Apr	Sales Returns	47
8 Apr	Sales	221	30 Apr	Balance c/d	752
22 Apr	Sales	395			
		799			799
1 May	Balance b/d	752			

10.2

Dr	Purchases Account		Cr
20-6		£	20-6		£

Dr				Purchases Account			Cr
20-6			£	20-6			£
1 Nov	Balance b/d		64,287	30 Nov	Balance c/d		71,007
30 Nov	Purchases Day Book		6,720				
			71,007				71,007
1 Dec	Balance b/d		71,007				

Dr				Purchases Returns Account			Cr
20-6			£	20-6			£
30 Nov	Balance c/d		1,509	1 Nov	Balance b/d		1,349
				30 Nov	Purchases Returns Day Book		160
			1,509				1,509
				1 Dec	Balance b/d		1,509

Dr				Value Added Tax Account			Cr
20-6			£	20-6			£
30 Nov	Purchases Day Book		1,176	1 Nov	Balance b/d		644
				30 Nov	Purchases Returns Day Book		28
				30 Nov	Balance c/d		504
			1,176				1,176
1 Dec	Balance b/d		504				

Dr				Rent Received Account			Cr
20-6			£	20-6			£
30 Nov	Balance c/d		4,500	1 Nov	Balance b/d		3,750
				14 Nov	Bank		375
				28 Nov	Bank		375
			4,500				4,500
				1 Dec	Balance b/d		4,500

Dr				Murray Limited			Cr
20-6			£	20-6			£
1 Nov	Balance b/d		15	8 Nov	Purchases		230
11 Nov	Purchases Returns		42	16 Nov	Purchases		315
30 Nov	Balance c/d		659	24 Nov	Purchases		171
			716				716
				1 Dec	Balance b/d		659

10.3 •   asset of bank increases by £8,000
capital increases by £8,000
asset £8,000 – liability £0 = capital £8,000

•   asset of computer increases by £4,000
asset of bank decreases by £4,000
asset £8,000 – liability £0 = capital £8,000

•   asset of bank increases by £3,000
liability of loan increases by £3,000
asset £11,000 – liability £3,000 = capital £8,000

•   asset of van increases by £6,000
asset of bank decreases by £6,000
asset £11,000 – liability £3,000 = capital £8,000

10.4

capital	£20,000
capital	£10,000
liabilities	£7,550
assets	£14,100
liabilities	£18,430
assets	£21,160

10.5 (a) - (b)   Office equipment has been bought for £2,000 and paid from the bank

(b) - (c)   Received a loan of £6,000, paid into the bank

(c) - (d)   Bought a van for £10,000, paying from the bank

(d) - (e)   Owner introduces £2,000 additional capital, paid into the bank

(e) - (f)   Loan repayment of £3,000 made from the bank

10.6

	CAPITAL EXPENDITURE	REVENUE EXPENDITURE
(a) purchase cost of vehicles	✓	
(b) rent paid on premises		✓
(c) payments for purchases		✓
(d) legal fees paid relating to the purchase of property	✓	
(e) cost of redecoration of the office		✓
(f) cost of installation of air-conditioning in the office	✓	
(g) wages cost of own employees used to build extension to the stockroom	✓	
(h) cost of installation and setting up of a new machine	✓	

10.7

	CAPITAL INCOME	REVENUE INCOME
(a) rent received		✓
(b) commission received		✓
(c) receipt from sale of old office equipment	✓	
(d) bank loan received	✓	
(e) receipts from sales		✓
(f) cash discount received		✓
(g) receipt from increase in owner's capital	✓	
(h) receipt from sale of property	✓	

CHAPTER 11: THE INITIAL TRIAL BALANCE

11.1 (b)

11.2 (c)

11.3

Trial balance of Jane Greenwell as at 31 March 20-9

Name of account	Dr £	Cr £
Bank		1,250
Purchases	850	
Petty cash	48	
Sales		1,940
Purchases returns		144
Payables		1,442
Equipment	2,704	
Van	3,200	
Inventory at 1 April 20-8	1,210	
Sales returns	90	
Receivables	1,174	
Wages	1,500	
Capital *(missing figure)*		6,000
	10,776	10,776

11.4

Account name	Amount £	Debit £	Credit £
Office equipment	12,246	12,246	
Bank (debit balance)	3,091	3,091	
Petty cash control	84	84	
Inventory	11,310	11,310	
Capital	22,823		22,823
Drawings	2,550	2,550	
VAT owing to HM Revenue & Customs	3,105		3,105
Loan from bank	8,290		8,290
Purchases ledger control	17,386		17,386
Sales ledger control	30,274	30,274	
Sales	82,410		82,410
Purchases	39,496	39,496	
Purchases returns	2,216		2,216
Sales returns	3,471	3,471	
Discount received	298		298
Discount allowed	517	517	
Wages	20,212	20,212	
Advertising	4,390	4,390	
Insurance	1,045	1,045	
Heating and lighting	1,237	1,237	
Rent and rates	4,076	4,076	
Travel costs	854	854	
Postages	721	721	
Telephone	954	954	
Totals		136,528	136,528

11.5

Account name	Amount £	Debit £	Credit £
Sales	101,269		101,269
Sales returns	3,476	3,476	
Purchases	54,822	54,822	
Purchases returns	4,107		4,107
Sales ledger control	25,624	25,624	
Purchases ledger control	18,792		18,792
Discount received	399		399
Discount allowed	210	210	
Rent and rates	3,985	3,985	
Advertising	4,867	4,867	
Insurance	1,733	1,733	
Wages	31,246	31,246	
Heating and lighting	3,085	3,085	
Postages	1,211	1,211	
Telephone	985	985	
Travel costs	2,311	2,311	
Miscellaneous expenses	107	107	
Capital	22,489		22,489
Vehicles	22,400	22,400	
Inventory	12,454	12,454	
Petty cash control	85	85	
Bank overdraft	6,291		6,291
VAT owing to HM Revenue & Customs	3,054		3,054
Loan from bank	12,200		12,200
Totals		168,601	168,601

Index